light candles...
not fires

Published by Mt. Nittany Press,
an imprint of Eifrig Publishing,
PO Box 66, Lemont, PA 16851.
Knobelsdorffstr. 44, 14059 Berlin, Germany

For information regarding permission, write to:
Rights and Permissions Department,
Eifrig Publishing,
PO Box 66, Lemont, PA 16851, USA.
permissions@eifrigpublishing.com, 814.954.9445.

Library of Congress Cataloging-in-Publication Data

Merritt, Andrew
  light candles...not fires, by Andrew Merritt
    p.   cm.

Paperback: ISBN 978-1-63233-326-1
Ebook: ISBN 978-1-63233-327-8

    1. Memoir 2. Self-help

    I. Merritt, Andrew, II. Title.

26 25 24 23 2022

5 4 3 2 1

Printed on acid-free paper. ∞

light candles... not fires

A single candle can light thousands of candles from the same flame without ever losing its beauty and brightness. For a fraction of a second the candle may slightly dim, but once the new candle is lit, the flame regains its intensity and burns more brightly. That is the amazing thing about candles, from one single candle thousands of lights may burn and light the way for others. Even cooler, from those thousands of candles, millions more candles can be lit and millions of people will be able to see more clearly.

We can be a candle. You get it, it's a metaphor. It's life and the ability to light the way or provide light to those in the dark. Lighting candles really costs us nothing. It's a kind word to someone struggling, it's a whisper of encouragement in the ear of your daughter as she prepares for the game. It's a quick stop at the store to buy flowers for your friend. It's a Dunkin Donuts gift card for coffee.

It's these acts of kindness that light people up.

Love people when they are at their worst
Lend a hand and a smile. Be first

You never know what struggles they face
Put yourself in their place

A smile and laugh may hide a lie
Life can be difficult they could be giving it a try

Know that those who offer a suggestion
Are offering a new direction

Not telling one how to act
But seeing the quality in you and showing a different track

Every day be kind
No matter how hard you may find

Have a beauty day

Love you both give em hell

(from a series of poems I send my daughters daily)

Everyday, I intentionally seek ways to help those who may be struggling for whatever reason. As a teacher, it tends to come naturally. It's not hard, and the value added is immeasurable.

Next time you get a chance, light a candle. Look for ways to lighten a load or ease a burden or offer encouragement. It's really that simple.

Forward

(this is not a typo, this is the way to live)

Much of what you will read in this book is deeply personal. Some of it has only been shared with family and close friends. As I write this, I am finding that what I thought would be a simple, "Hey listen to this, I have something to say" has turned into an examination of my life and forced me to ask, "Am I good enough? Am I a Good Man?"

This is really not a book, but rather a collection of experiences, thoughts and ideas cobbled together in no particular way, especially focused on life and my experiences and my continual push forward.

The editors who read this writing described it as a "memoir, personal journal and life advice book." It may be all of these things, or something else.

While I may care about these stories, thoughts and ideas and find them valuable, I don't know if you will. You will decide if they resonate with you. You are the one who decides if reading this is valuable. For me, I must trust the reader and believe this is valuable.

As I read and reread this writing, I vacillated between, "Why am I doing this?" to "This is awesome!"

At a minimum, this process has been cathartic. And that is something.

I am a teacher by profession and I believe it is who I am, not what I do. In school I am outgoing and easily interact with students and staff. It is something of a facade, as I am far more reserved in my personal life. I normally spend my non-school time in my safe and warm cave, believing that I am so smart. I am unaccustomed to putting myself out there, intentionally making myself vulnerable. With this writing, I am choosing to leave the cave and step into the light.

I read a lot and believe that most non-fiction books are, at a minimum, twice as long as they need to be. Sometimes I think writers write to make themselves sound brilliant; the word "pedantic" comes to mind. So, I won't do that, mostly because I am not brilliant.

My promise: I will do all I can to limit any superfluous explanations and cut right to the heart of the matter.

I would not be a good teacher if I did not ask you to do something at the end of each section. No worries, it's not an essay or math. "Time to Reflect" is a chance for you to, well, reflect, to consider how these words and your life connect.

Some of the activities may be difficult, others easy. They are meant to help you make sense or practice some of the things I am writing about. They are tasks meant to challenge you and your values. They are meant to help you reflect and ask yourself, "Who am I?"

To really grow and be our best selves, we may need to squirm a bit. I am not asking you to eat worms, but some of you may prefer that to the task you are asked to perform.

This writing is not intended as a sit down, read-straight-through book. I suggest it's best consumed in small bites so you can then take some time to reflect. Also, with the exception of the last chapter, feel free to roam around and read sections that appeal to you. This writing doesn't build on itself, one section doesn't necessarily lead to the next.

Throughout the reading you will come across short poems. These are poems I send to my daughters every day. Some are serious, others silly. The poems are the basis for some of the topics you will read about. For nearly four years I have written a poem almost every weekday. I've found them to be a way to send short thoughts that hopefully give my daughters something to think about or at least smile about.

So who am I to write a book?

Life circumstances brought me here. These experiences pushed me to slow down and appreciate what I have. Reading has broadened my world and brought new meaning. I delved into the world of Buddhism, Stoicism, mindfulness and just about anything else I can get my hands on to read or listen to via podcasts that challenge who I am and everything I believe.

I have read everything by Eckhart Tolle, JK Zinn, Thich Nhat Hahn, Anthony De Mello, James Baldwin, Pema Chodron, Ryan Holiday, Ta'nehisi Coates, Red Cloud, Humble the Poet, Viktor Frankl, Khalil Gibran, Marcus Aurelius, Seneca, Plato...the list goes on and on.

Through this reading and continual reflection, I have reached the conclusion that life is meant to be celebrated, not mourned; to be seized, not to float aimlessly within; to add value, not to take; to do good, not to harm; to own our actions, not to deflect; to drive, not be driven.

So, I offer you my thoughts on life; take them for what they are worth. Perhaps you may find a few nuggets of wisdom, or perhaps you may find yourself wondering why you are reading it at all and hoping you can get your money back?

In either case, I declare victory, because my goal is to make you think, challenge, wonder, say "hmmmm", laugh, cry, relate, reject. To feel, not simply exist. I do not pretend to have all the answers to the challenges life throws at us but I do have life experiences and perhaps you can take from those.

The highlight of my day
Thinking of good words to say

I send you only love and kindness
Hoping your day is the bess (my poem my word)

Focus on the now, not what if
Be present not stiff

Do what you can all day
Try only right thoughts and right words to say

Think how you can be the light
More kind less fight

Have a beauty day

Love you both give em hell

The book...

Note: Unless otherwise noted, all names have been changed for individual protection and privacy.

Topics:

"

The warrior, for us, is one who sacrifices himself for the good of others. His task is to take care of the elderly, the defenseless, those who can not provide for themselves, and above all, the children, the future of humanity.

Sitting Bull
Hunkpapa Sioux

So, why write this book now?

Part I: An angry young man and a couple of very sharp knives

I am just a guy who, for the past couple years, dealt with some pretty scary stuff. Yes, much of it's the typical stuff that a father and husband of a beautiful wife and wonderful, smart kids deals with: college decisions, cars, drivers licenses, aging parents, death of a sibling, etc.

But there have also been tough familial situations that have pushed me into some extreme anxiety-laden grounds. Throw in a large dose of serious chronic pain from a bad hip. Add to all this a PTSD event that left me wondering, "What the hell just happened? What the hell was that?"

The PTSD event, the short version:
A former student was struggling with addiction and was met with an intervention that went horribly sideways.

The PTSD event, the long version:
I got a call from a parent of a student I had in class a few years prior. He told me his son was struggling with substance abuse and erratic behavior most likely caused by drugs and alcohol. He asked if I would be willing to take part in an intervention. He said his son had spoken very highly of me and he thought I, along with his family members, may be able to help his son get the help he needed.

The father had already contracted with an alleged well-known and well-respected intervention specialist. She was driving into town the next day and wanted to meet all the people involved in the intervention to provide an overview of the process. I agreed and went to the meeting.

I should have recognized something was amiss when the interventionist sat through the entire meeting petting a small dog she held firmly in her lap. She assured us all that her dog was part of the process. She said no person, who was the focus of the intervention, had ever reacted negatively to her or the dog.

Well that was about to change.

The meeting with the interventionist and her dog concluded after two hours and we agreed to meet at the father's home at 8:30 AM the next morning. It was to be me, the father, the mother, an aunt who had flown in to be there, a trusted family friend, the grandfather, and an uncle; a total of seven family and friends plus the interventionist and her dog.

The young man who was the focus of the intervention was still asleep so the interventionist and her dog went to wake him up. Remember. He has no idea what is occurring, that an intervention is taking place. This young man also has no idea who this lady is or why she is there with a dog and why she is waking him up and asking him to come upstairs.

Somehow she was able to awaken him and get him to come upstairs. As soon as he turned the corner into the room where we all had gathered, the look on his face said all I needed to know:

This was not going to go well.

He said, "What the fuck is going on? Why are all of you here? What the hell is happening?"

The interventionist quietly explained that out of an abundance of love and care we all had come to ask him to get help with his addiction and behavior. She had arranged a drug and alcohol rehab placement out of state and all he had to do was say yes. First though, she said, he should hear how much we loved him and how much we wanted him to get help.

Yeah, that did not go well either.

Initially he agreed to listen for a few minutes and sat beside me on the couch. After a few of us had spoken, he reached his limit and stood up and demanded we all leave his house. (That is the polite version.)

He then headed to the kitchen and we could hear him rummaging through a drawer. We asked the father what he was doing and he responded, "He is looking for a knife."

It was only then the father told us that his son, when enraged and out of control, would take a very large knife and repeatedly drive it into the door frame outside the home. I thought, "Why does he have a knife that an enraged, out-of-control 20-year-old had access to? Man, you should be hiding the knives."

Throughout this episode the interventionist was silent, not a word, only petting her dog. After about a minute the young man appeared in the doorway between the living area and the kitchen, knife in hand, and said quite plainly, "Get the fuck out of my house." He turned and headed out the back door. We all heard the door slam. Fortunately he left the knife on the counter and we saw him skate away on his longboard.

All the interventionist said was, "Well, that has never happened before."

I did not believe her.

The father took the knife and hid it away.

The group began talking in an attempt to figure out next steps. Should we look for him, should we heed his advice and leave, should we wait for him? The interventionist said nothing except, again, that this had never happened before.

I still did not believe her.

We stayed.

After about 45 minutes he returned, saw us all still there and again said, "Get the fuck out of my house." He now had another knife, as large as the first and just as scary looking. I thought, what is it with this family and knives?

This is when an already dangerous and volatile situation became a threat to kill someone. He pointed at various family members and said he would be better off without them. I remember he pointed at me and said, "Mr. Merritt you are OK, I am OK you are here, I got nothing against you."

Then he said perhaps we would all be better off without him and went on a riff about how suicide is noble and sometimes the best option. That people who kill themselves are brave, etc., and then he headed into the garage with that very large and very nasty looking knife in hand. The last thing I remember the interventionist saying was that the father should call the police.

We could hear him continue his rant as he knocked things over in the garage, which was scary enough but was far better than the silence a suicide would bring. If he were shouting and breaking stuff, he was not harming himself.

Something had to be done. The uncle and I spoke about what to do next; the interventionist and her dog were in deep water, far over their heads. We could hear him but we could not see him. The police were on the way and this could become deadly if we did not act quickly.

Since I was the only non-family member present and was least likely to be stabbed, and the young man said "I was OK," I was chosen. I want to say I volunteered to go in the garage, but as the situation was rapidly deteriorating, I went. The how or why didn't matter.

Here is what I knew:
He had taken a knife, a rather large knife, and a nasty "get the fuck out of my house" attitude into the garage and shut the door. My mission was to somehow get into that garage and keep an eye on him to ensure he would not come back into the house. At the same time, I needed to be ready to act if he turned the knife on himself.

As if I had ever done this before. A walk in the park.

I spent five years in the military, and although never in combat, I did face some fairly stressful situations with large automatic weapons. But I was never as fearful about my personal safety as I was at that moment.

I knocked on the garage door and announced myself and told him I wanted

to talk with him, that was it. I was not going to do anything else.
I slowly opened the door, announced I was coming into the garage, not knowing what was on the other side.

We stood face to face, both of us crying, me pleading with him not to harm himself and him continuing to say it's the best option.

The police arrived very quickly. From my position, looking into the garage, I could see them and he could not. The emergency vehicles arrived without lights and sirens. I saw a police SUV, followed by an ambulance, followed by several police cars and other SUVs. The cavalry had arrived.

He must have seen me glance away and look out the window. He turned his head and saw the police cars and a couple officers stealthily approaching the garage.

He looked at me and asked, "Why are the police here? Are they here for me?" Before I could answer, he said, "They must be here for me, I have to go talk to these police officers."

The change was literally that quick. That is exactly how he said it.

He put the knife on the floor of the garage and walked past me and greeted the police officers. I waited a few seconds to ensure he was far enough away from me and the knife and then I picked the knife up and asked the officer near the door what I should do with it. He took it from me.
I was glad.

The Officer In Charge was an officer I knew for many years and when I saw her, I knew this situation was under control.

Good news, it all worked out. He went to rehab, got some help, and graduated with honors from college. I bumped into him recently, he is doing very well. He looks fantastic. He is healthy and clean. I am very proud of him.

As for the interventionist, I never heard about her again. I do hope she's found another line of work.

Part II: Ugly, dark and scary

For me, the intervention did not end as well. Just as the young man was struggling to get things right, I began to struggle. The experience with the intervention was the final event in a downward spiral I didn't realize I was caught in. My world began to close in.

A few weeks after the intervention, I was driving to visit my mom in Alexandria Bay, New York, and suddenly I had the scariest and strangest thoughts pop into my head.

Suddenly, out of nowhere, my brain was sending me ugly, dark and scary thoughts. I had strange thoughts before but never like this. No matter how hard I tried, I could not push them out of my brain. They scared me to the point I thought I was losing my mind. What I later learned was that the more I tried to push them out, the stronger they became. Eckhart Tolle would say, "What we resist, persists."

For a few days, while in New York, I wrestled with them and when I returned home they didn't go away. They were violent, crossing into suicidal. I was terrified. I did not know what to do.

Finally, on the Saturday after I returned from New York, I could no longer take it and I asked my wife to take me to the hospital for a psychological evaluation. She knew I was struggling with something but did not know what it was.

I did not tell her what was going on in my head. How could I? How could I tell the people I love more than anything in the world that I had these ugly, dark and scary thoughts.

At the hospital they ran all the tests. I spoke a couple times with a doctor and a mental health crisis counselor. The doctors found nothing.

Prior to sending me home, my wife and children were allowed to come into the exam room. The doctors said they saw nothing to hold me and recommended I get an evaluation from a psychologist as soon as possible. It was then I told my family what was going on in my brain. In our 27 years together I never had seen the concern, fear and confusion in her as I saw in that second. I can still recall the look on her face. I never want to see it again. It was the lowest point of my life.

At a minimum, my family knew what was going on in my brain. To make my wife and our kids feel safer I offered to go and stay somewhere else. I wanted to give my family time to make sense of what I was experiencing. As worried as she was, she wanted me to stay with her and the kids. I was glad and relieved.

Our oldest daughter was a junior in college, a social work major. She immediately reached out to an acquaintance of mine, a psychologist. I don't know what she said to him, but she set up an appointment for me for that Monday.

When I arrived home from the hospital, I began reading, literally, and haven't stopped. I had to figure out what was going on in my brain and I found it in a book called DARE by Barry McDonagh. He explained the idea of "Intrusive Thoughts."

Intrusive thoughts are random thoughts that come out of nowhere and explode in brains like bombs. Some of them may be sexual, some may be criminal, like weirdly thinking what it would be like to rob a bank. Others are about doom and gloom, perhaps fearing you will crash your car or get run over by a bus. Intrusive thoughts are not phobias. They are exactly what they are titled. Oftentimes they appear in people who are exactly the opposite of what the thoughts manifest.

My intrusive thoughts were ugly and dark, and why this was so scary is that I am not in any way a dark person; actually I would consider myself to be far more positive, upbeat and kind.

It is estimated that 80% of all people have some form of intrusive thoughts. Most simply write them off as, "well, that was weird" and move on. That is how I normally dealt with them. In other situations these thoughts "stick" and can be debilitating. In this case, that was me. Every effort to push them away made them stronger.

I knew I would never act on these thoughts but not understanding them and where they came from crippled me and made me sick. As I read more, I understood more and eventually was able to regain control.

My wife took me to the first therapist appointment on that Monday. The work with the therapist was invaluable. I was able to speak with him in a way I normally do not with anyone else. I remember telling him, "I am fucking scared to death." I never speak like that in conversation.

The psychologist asked my wife to join us at the end of the first session. He assured her I was OK, some anxiety and mild depression, but nothing that could not be addressed. I had some work to do and I would need some time and more sessions to help figure this all out.

His assurances were what I and she needed to hear.

On that Saturday at the hospital, I saw concern, fear, and confusion on my wife's face. On Monday, in the psychologist's office, I still saw concern, but the fear was now relief and her smile returned. She held my hand as we left, I needed that. We were going to be OK.

After some more sessions with the psychologist, we figured the cause of the intrusive thoughts was a combination of an ongoing very difficult family situation, a physical crisis (the severe pain from a bad hip), and the student/ knife intervention.

It was, as Mike, my psychologist called it, a perfect storm. Individually the events, the PTSD, the hip pain and familial strife are more easily handled, but nearly simultaneously, they created a trifecta of trouble that manifested in my mental health crisis.

Working with the psychologist and sharing my feelings with my wife and kids was one of the hardest things I have ever done, and at the same time, one of the most valuable things I have ever done. I was open with everyone. I knew that I would need my family to get through this. I am better for it, stronger, wiser, healthier, more informed, and more empathetic.

Many people, especially men, wrongly believe that seeking help is a sign of weakness. It is not. Knowing you are struggling and asking for help is a sign of strength. We all have far too much to lose to NOT ask for help.

The physical crisis.

For many months leading up to the intervention, the mental health crisis and the intrusive thoughts, I was in severe physical pain. I needed a hip replacement; it was rapidly deteriorating. The hip pain, I believe, more than anything else, was the biggest part of the perfect storm that caused the mental health crisis.

The two month time from late June when the intervention took place to late August when the hip surgery took place seemed like a year. Pain from my hip made me someone I didn't like. Someone my wife and children didn't deserve. I had never been so mentally confused and fearful. I was physically ill, I could not eat. I lost 18 pounds.

Fortunately, I was working with a psychologist to make sense of it all. More importantly, I had a wife and two adult kids who knew I was struggling, both mentally and physically, and stuck with me. I was also fortunate enough to have the means to get the necessary surgery.

Pain is a dangerous thing:
- I am not talking about stubbing your toe pain that hurts and is painful but soon fades. I am talking about chronic pain. The kind that slowly creeps into your life over weeks, months, and years. Pain that initially can be controlled with a couple of aspirin or Tylenol. As time goes on, extra doses become common or the addition of a different OTC and instead of every 8 hours it is now every 6 hours or every 4 hours.
- Chronic pain is insidious, like a boa constrictor that slowly envelopes and then consumes its prey. Pretty soon OTC medications are impotent/worthless but they begin to cause other medical conditions and you begin to look for other ways to numb the pain.

I remember waking up from the anesthesia in my hospital room, and for the first time in months being hungry and feeling no pain. My wife was sitting, waiting for me in my hospital room and had a peppermint patty as a snack for herself. I asked for a bite. I don't like peppermint patties. I ate it all.

My learning:

This entire series of events taught me the danger of pain, both physical and mental. I recognized how easy it would be to search for an easy out, anything to take the pain away: a bottle, pills, a pipe, a needle, or worse. In our society today many are struggling with internal pain. We need to help each other.

I don't believe any person sets out to be an alcoholic or heroin addict. People end up in these situations because life is hard and they need a coping mechanism, they are afraid, or they may not know where to turn for help or admit they need help. They may not have a support network. I was fortunate to have a support network.

If you're reading this and are struggling with a mental health crisis and considering harming yourself. DO NOT. You are not alone.

Stop reading right now and call a friend, reach out and ask for help. Or call the National Suicide Prevention Lifeline: 800-273-8255.

If you have a friend struggling with a mental health crisis, get them help. If it is severe enough, find a local mental health crisis line and YOU call for them.

Time to reflect:
Consider one event in your life that impacted you so strongly you remember it as if it happened this morning. How has that event affected you? Has it made you stronger or limited your potential? If it has limited you, what are possible ways to overcome its impact?

My early years

I was born into a middle-class family. I was the fourth of five kids. My older sister was the oldest and smartest of the bunch; and then there were my two older brothers and younger sister.

Like most young people I was fairly oblivious to the world around me; I had some good friends, food, a bed, two parents and always something to do. My parents owned ten acres of farm fields and every year from the age of six I spent many hours planting tomatoes, peppers, corn, etc. and even many more hours pulling weeds, picking vegetables, and selling them at our roadside stand.

As a young person, I resented working in the fields as it conflicted with baseball or playing with my friends. What I could not know then was that the work I was doing and the responsibility put upon me at a young age made me a better and more responsible person as an adult.

The cool thing was that I learned to drive at a very young age.

You see, my dad also owned a towing business and when he towed in a car that was really no longer road safe, oftentimes the owner would sign it over to my dad in lieu of payment and it would become a "lot car." During picking season, we would drive the car through the rows and fill the trunk and back seat with corn. We would then take it to the roadside stand, unload the corn and sell it. This roadside stand paid for all of our school clothing, a family vacation and a trip to the horse racing track. Yeah, my parents took four kids—and eventually five—to the track.

After the growing season was over, my brothers and I would rip around the fields in our "lot car." No surprise then that by the age of 13, I was driving. My sister and brothers were getting summer jobs, and I was left to do much of the planting, weeding, picking, and selling. Driving made the work far more fun.

In July of 1976, my middle-class existence took a swift downturn. My dad lost his business. He owned an auto repair shop and gas station in our town. Due to some bookkeeping issues resulting in a tax snafu, the state of New York took the business. My dad was embarrassed and I knew things were tough, but my parents did the best they could to shield me from the tumult.

From that time on my parents struggled financially. I watched and helped as best I could as he rebuilt his business, literally from the ground up, at our house. Every day for the rest of that summer, my dad and a small construction company were busy building the structure that would come to be known as "Merritt's Garage." It took shape over three months and by September it was open.

Writing about this, it just now struck me: how did we survive financially over those months? I will never know the answer but I believe it was my mom's dad, my grandfather, who kept us afloat. It was never mentioned.

Because of the financial limitations placed on my parents as my dad regrew his business, anything new was limited, including things like shoes, birthday and Christmas gifts. In retrospect, the gifts I received during those years were the best and most meaningful. I know what it's like to not have the newest clothing, gadgets or toys. I understand the value of hand me downs and clothes that "you will grow into."

I know what it's like to have homemade Christmas gifts. Gifts from Christmas of 1976 consisted of a homemade personalized bath towel and a few other small items. None of us complained.

These experiences made me more creative and appreciative of what I did have.

I look back on those days as a boy and eventually as a young man with fondness and respect. From those days and experiences I learned what it means to work hard and to value the little things. My mom and dad were great examples of this for me.

Even after his business was up and running, my dad worked two jobs: he ran his auto repair shop by day, and from November through April he worked at our local township road maintenance building overnights as a radio dispatcher calling in road crews as necessary for snow plowing and road salting/sanding. My mom took on a full time job as a weigh master at a gravel pit where she earned the nickname "Gravel Annie", she had her own hardhat.

It seemed natural for me to have several jobs beginning at the age of 13. In addition to working in the corn and tomato fields, I worked at a sports complex lining fields and providing general maintenance. I also picked up garbage and was a flagger on a road crew. And after a year of college, I enlisted in the military.

These are the experiences and memories that helped to shape me. While I may have gone without the best new things, I can genuinely say I have never known what it feels like to be without love. That love was expressed in countless ways—rarely words, and far more actions.

My family was never overt about saying "I love you." But it was in everything my parents did. The sacrifice, the showing up at events, the few dollars slipped into your hand as you headed out the door.

I knew I was loved but it was also nice to hear.

Because I rarely heard it, I learned to say it, to plainly and clearly tell those that are vital to me how much they mean. This is not reserved only for family members, but anyone I feel a real connection to, both men and women alike. I believe if we are more willing to recognize and show how important people are to us, the less struggle we will have as a society. You know someone has your back. By the end of my parents' lives, an "I love you" finished every conversation with both my mom and dad.

I hope my words can help people understand that we all are worthy of love and we all can give love, we just have to be open to it.

Time to reflect:
Take a few minutes to think about your formative years, the things you did, the people you knew and how they influenced you either positively or negatively. Consider how those years and those experiences made you who you are today.

"The two most important days in your life are the day you are born and the day you find out why."
~Mark Twain

Most of us have heard this pearl from Twain or at least some version of it. We all know we were born but how many of us really know the "why" part? We often confuse our version of success for the why, substituting expectations for nice cars, houses, lots of money for the why.

You want nice things and lots of money, become a stockbroker or go into finance. You probably will get those nice things, but for many, this focus may leave a void for the things money cannot replace: Doing good and adding value to the world. This can mean the world writ large—like the universe or the planet; or it can mean your world, your family, home, neighborhood, or community.

My "why" moment came to me completely by accident. I have spent the time since figuring out how to operationalize it.

I always thought of myself as a decent human being, kind, thoughtful, compassionate, etc. These attributes were ingrained in me by my parents and if you know my wife she would never be with any person less than that. I am also a teacher, so by default, these are traits - either inherent or learned - that defined me.

It was April of 2004, my mom and dad were visiting us for the weekend to see our girls play baseball. It was a Saturday morning and as we were getting ready to go to the game, the phone rang and I answered it. It was a student of mine who lived fairly close to us. He explained that he and his dad had gotten into a fight and that he needed some help. I told him to come to our house and I would help him sort it out. He arrived about 10 minutes later and as he got out of his truck, I immediately noticed the redness on his cheeks, bruising on his neck and arms; this had been a serious fight.

He came into the house and we talked. I told him I had to report this to our county Children and Youth Services office and needed to make some calls. I called a school counselor and the counselor told me to get some pictures and document the event. In the course of my conversation with the counselor, I could hear the young man and my dad talking. It was largely small talk.

Then it happened. My "why" moment.

My dad, a former AAA baseball player, police officer, ARMY Korean War veteran, truck driver, and small business owner said to him - and I will never forget it: "Son (he called every young man son), you will be OK. My son will take care of you, he is a good man."

BAM!

There it was. My "why"! After 42 years of thinking I knew my purpose, it suddenly became clear. I had military service and was a teacher. Those were my identities and I thought those were my whys. It wasn't until my dad distilled my life's purpose into five words - "he is a good man" - that I got it. The words rolled out so genuinely and easily. My dad believed in me and my ability to help this young man at his lowest point. I knew he meant it.

A bit about me and my dad...

For most of my early life, until about the age of 19, I really did not think my dad liked me. I knew he loved me, but was not quite sure of the "like" part. I was a thinker, more of an academic, and despite the work I grew up doing, I did not like to get my hands dirty. My older brothers spent far more time with him going on tow calls and working in the auto repair shop. I was jealous of their relationship with him and he and I battled quite frequently.

It was not until I was 19 and I joined the military did I realize that he did, in fact, like me. I spent a great deal of time with him the summer before I left for basic training. While in basic training, HE wrote me letters. And HE sent me money when I knew for certain he and my mom could have used the 5 bucks.

After I left the military, while finishing college, my dad and I became best friends, and an unspoken mutual respect developed. I sensed his pride for me. Perhaps it was our shared military experience. I really do not know. More likely, I grew up.

I asked him to be my best man at my wedding; he declined only because he thought I should ask my brother.

On that Saturday morning in April 2004, my dad's words hit me in a way that I could not have imagined. My dad, a man who accomplished more in his life than I could ever achieve, a guy who raised five successful children, a guy who worked two jobs after his business closed, a guy that sacrificed sleep, money, and even health to make sure we had all we needed, thought I was a good man?

That was my "why." To be a Good Man, always.

Literally, since that moment, I measure everything I do, every action, every interaction, with the "Good Man" rule. In all honesty I am still not sure I have a full understanding of what it means to be a "Good Man," but I have come to see that at its core, it's about looking out for those who cannot look out for themselves.

It took me six years to share that story with other people. Now at the end of each semester of my class, I share that story with my students and challenge them to be "Good Men." Of course I am not just talking to the young men. I am speaking to all of the students. They all understand they have an obligation to be "Good People." To defend those who cannot defend themselves, to open a door for someone carrying a heavy load (better yet, offer to carry the load), to offer words of encouragement to someone who is struggling, to throw a rope to someone in a hole (better yet, to join them in the hole and lead them out), to do good, to be people of character and integrity, to fight the fights that must be fought.

Give em hell!

What is your "why?" What is your "Good Man" moment? You never know when or where it will come from. It could be the 2 AM phone call of an old friend asking for help, it could be your mom or dad struggling with the demands of growing old, it could be defending a child from an abusive situation or simply spending time with someone in need.

There is no doubt, your "why" moment will come. Don't be afraid, lean into it, embrace it, wrap yourself in it and live it. Too many people spend their lives running away from the tough stuff. It's easier to not get involved, to look away, to live in fear.

Good men answer the call.

My dad epitomized the Stoic pillars of wisdom, courage, justice and temperance. My Stoic friends will get it; for the rest, look it up.
My dad used to drop me off at my soccer games and as I climbed out of his truck he would simply say, "Give em hell." Perhaps that best summarizes who he was and what being a "Good Man" is all about. I have "Give em hell" tattooed on my chest with his birth date under it.

Time to reflect: Push yourself to identify your "why" moment. When identified, ask yourself if you have lived up to its meaning? As I said, I am still unsure I have a full understanding of its meaning and I wonder if I'm fully living up to it. It's OK if you believe you have not. Identifying it is what is most critical, living it is the next step.

"Holding onto anger is like drinking poison and expecting the other person to die" ~ *Gautama Buddha*

This quote has been attributed to many people, but for those who study Buddhism, it definitely may have been said by the Buddha.

In the film American History X, Derek Vinyard, played by Edward Norton, is an angry young man—angry at the world for the murder of his father, a firefighter, who died after being shot by black drug dealers while putting out a fire. Derek quickly is sucked into the world of hatred, Neo-Nazism, white supremacy and all the ugliness and violence that accompanies it. He is eventually convicted of manslaughter in the death of a gang member and finds himself in prison. In prison his beliefs about white supremacy are challenged and he understands the damage that the intense anger and hate have done to him.

In prison, he sees the hypocrisy in blaming others for his lot in life while, at the same time, working with them in illegal prison activities. Derek let anger and resentment be the poison that carried him to prison and discovered that an open mind and education would carry him out.

For those who like movies with happy endings about redemption, this movie is not for you.

All of us carry the weight of anger and resentment. They weigh us down like lead. We spend time lamenting and blaming, continuing to drink the poison, somehow thinking it will get better. It won't. Period. End.

The only way to overcome anger and resentment is to let it go, to release the power it holds over us.

For many years, even prior to my study of Eastern cultures, I did my best not to let anger drive my emotions. I told people they didn't have the power to make me hate or act in a negative fashion. I was not always successful in making this true for myself, but I was aware.

About 15 years ago, one of my students confided in me that her stepfather had sexually assaulted her from about the age of 9 until about the age of 16. She had found the courage to tell me and another teacher. As mandatory reporters, we reported what she told us. This young woman found the courage to file a police report and her stepfather was arrested. She was taking her power back.

As the legal case developed, she was alone. Her family turned on her and sided with the man. This was an intense time and I would often check in with her to see how she was doing. I noticed that she was gaining strength and confidence. Her zest for life increased, and she was having more good days than bad. She was now in charge. My anger was just beginning.

About 3 months later the case was ready for trial. I spoke with her quite frequently as the trial date came closer. I told her that I, along with the other teacher, would do anything we could to help her. The young woman asked us to come to the courthouse for the trial. She needed friendly and supportive faces in the gallery. Of course we agreed to be there to support her.

I had attended a couple of student court cases before— child custody, small crimes, etc., but nothing like this.

I spoke with the young woman at the courthouse and told her that when it got tough, and I knew it would be tough, to look at me and the other teacher. Take strength from us and know we were there only for her.

I knew that in these cases, the victim had to tell the court what the perpetrator did to her, in detail. If you never have to be part of this, you are fortunate. It is ugly, and far worse for the victim as they are forced to replay the events in front of many people. My anger continued to grow.

The handcuffed stepfather was brought into the courtroom and took his seat about 15 feet away from me on my left. Since this was a juvenile case, we were in an auxiliary courtroom, away from any media. It was a very small room. I can still see him sitting at the defense table, rolling his eyes and smiling, acting as if this were a waste of his time.

The young woman was the only witness and was called to speak in detail about the assaults on her. The DA had given her a small doll to hold as a comfort item; she clutched it tightly as the questioning began. The DA also reminded her that she would have to give detailed descriptions of what he did to her. She was ready and the questioning began.

The DA asked her to explain when the assaults began and what her stepfather did to her. She began by talking about how when he was not working, he often found ways to be alone with her. She was 9.

The DA asked her to explain what he did when they were alone. She then gave graphic details about how he would burn her with cigarettes and then rape her. He threatened to harm her more if she told others about the burning and rape. It was early on in the questioning that this young woman who had regained her strength as a 17-year-old young woman, reverted to a 9-year-old little girl. Her voice changed, her demeanor changed. Before our eyes, she became that 9-year-old girl again. She pulled the doll closer and cried. I cried too and the anger in me raged. I was seething.

I remember looking at the stepfather sitting there with a smirk on his face, obviously enjoying forcing her to relive the assaults. He was taking pleasure in this testimony. I could feel my blood boil.

I recall thinking to myself, "I could jump this railing and at least get a few good shots in before the bailiff or sheriffs could get to me. I may not end him but he would feel the anger and rage I was feeling and the young woman knew someone had her back."

I was feeling anger like I had never felt. Over three months of knowing what this person had done to her was coming to the fore. Perhaps it was knowing many others who had been assaulted. I wanted to act.

I looked at her and I looked at him. It was odd, but at that moment, I heard the young woman's voice change; once again, it became stronger. The DA continued the questioning and she was now in charge. The 9-year-old little girl was replaced by a strong confident young woman I knew from

3 months previous. The DA asked her about each assault, and there were many. The DA asked her to point at the person who did it to her and she confidently looked and pointed at him. She had found her feet, and was now in charge.

With each question she became stronger and by the end of her very lengthy testimony, she was the boss. She had taken her power back.

As I reflect on that day, I know it was me who took strength from her. I see that my anger, rage and hate could have pushed me to do something that would have only added to an already intense situation. That my hatred nearly made me someone I am not. No good would have come from it, I may have felt better for a few minutes, but nothing more, and would have been arrested for assault. Her testimony, power and strength did far more than I could ever do.

In reality, there is no getting even. Anger only begets anger and hate only begets hate. And in some cases, it may get you arrested.

There is a story of two concentration camp inmates standing at the barbed wire fence of the camp. One of the men suddenly breaks into prayer, thanking god. His friend stops him and says, "My friend are you crazy? All around us are men who will kill us for simply looking the wrong way, they are murdering our friends and family, they have vicious dogs, they turn loose on us for sport. Why are you thanking god?" His friend answered simply, "I am thanking god for not making me like them."

While we all cannot be as strong and resolute as those who have survived the most horrific life experiences, we can try. We can learn and take strength from them. Their strength can make us better people.

We can be aware, we can remind ourselves each day that getting even only ups the ante. That sometimes the strongest person is the one who can point at her attacker, or walk away, or put down the weapon, not be driven to hate. For in reality, when we feed the anger, we become them. We become those we hate.

In the film 42, Branch Rickey demands Jackie Robinson be stronger than those who hurl racial epithets at him and threaten him and his family.

Robinson in pure emotion challenges Rickey and says "Don't you want someone strong enough to fight back?" Rickey responds, "I want a man strong enough NOT to fight back."

Be THAT person. The one who walks away, the one who stops talking. Be the peacemaker.

Let go or be dragged.

Time to reflect: Think of a time when you "drank the poison." How did it feel to let that anger drive you? How did it feel when you were finally able to let it go? If you have yet to let go, do so now.

"Don't chase the arsonist."
Thich Nhat Hahn

Better yet, don't be one. We all know that person or people that for whatever reason thrive on making others upset, lighting them on fire. They push you until you explode with anger or run away.

These people are arsonists.

I have never understood why people feel the need to treat others in this manner. I suppose it's about power and somehow finding their own value by demeaning and mocking others.

I've lived through arson. This was my familial crisis.

I have a brother, who, for many years at every family gathering, tormented, tortured, mocked and belittled my younger sister, Sally.

She is very active in animal rescue, with particular attention to and care for cats.

Sally devoted her entire life to protecting and providing for thousands of homeless and abandoned cats, in some cases sacrificing her own health to rescue feral cats.

She uses her own money to have them spayed or neutered and then finds families that meet her strict guidelines for their new home. Her work is thankless, admirable and noble. Fortunately her husband, Jon, although allergic, is right alongside her, providing encouragement and a home to sometimes up to 17 cats. He is the litter box guy, cleaning them everyday; a kind-hearted person who champions the underdog.

I am in awe of their work and dedication. Sally now has her own non-profit whose mission is to educate, empower and support the community members who care for free-roaming community cats through targeted TNVR (Trap, Neuter, Vaccinate, Return) practices.

The brother I referred to, on the other hand, somehow finds her work especially unworthy and continually mocks her efforts. I have heard it all, the dead cat "jokes," the waste of money comments, the "get a real job" remarks. It's deliberate and mean.

The disrespect and degradation always began the same way. A seemingly off-handed comment that gets no response leads to the next more pointed, "You know the only good cat is a dead cat." And the match is lit, but it doesn't stop there. He was just getting started. If the desired reaction still didn't occur, the next statement is meant as a flamethrower.

"Why do you waste your time and money on cats? You can't even work and you waste all this money on cats."

Now the house is fully engulfed and my sister, the person who devoted her life to championing the underdog, would flee the scene. The arsonist stands by with a gleeful smile. Mission accomplished.

I admired Jon's restraint. And to the good fortune of my brother, Jon never engaged him. (Jon is very fit.) Although I am very much a pacifist, if I'm being honest, a throw down would have been fun to watch. The smart money was on Jon.

My sister came to realize that this person is not a kind human being and she is thankful she is not him. His deliberate cruelty can not hurt her anymore. She has learned to let go.

I challenged him several times on the comments about my sister and her noble work, to no avail. He would complain my sister did not attend a family function and I would respond, "Why should she? Every time you interact with her you tear her down."

His response was always, "Why can't she take a joke?"

It was not funny.

I was not immune from the flamethrower. He took a different approach with me. Toward me, his barbs were about family. It was about how I did not visit enough (we lived about four hours away). How my parents cried and felt betrayed that somehow I had picked my wife's family over my own. This was not true.

As my mother's health had deteriorated, she moved in with his family. The new complaint was we did not make the now seven-hour trip often enough.

No matter how much I explained our very different life circumstances, it was never enough. The attacks were vicious, personal, and relentless, with another family member joining in on occasion.

My wife could spot it in a second. If one of his emails or texts came through, it would show on my face. Or I would find myself internalizing the anger and it spilling out in unintended ways.

At one point, I asked him directly why he disliked me so much, why was he so vicious toward me? He responded in a lengthy email detailing things from our childhood and the nearly 40 years since. He mentioned events of which I had no control or recollection. He was keeping score of all of my failings, or at least what he perceived as my failings. I responded that this must be tearing him up and recommended he talk with someone about his feelings. I do hope he has done that. That much anger and hate will destroy a person.

The arsonist is at their happiest when you are at your most miserable and vulnerable. The most serious and dangerous thing is that your negative reactions to any attack can have serious negative consequences for those whom you care about and love. There is a domino effect.

It has taken me several years to get to the point of accepting there is little anyone can say or do that will change the arsonist, but what we all can learn is to not chase the arsonist. It's a hard lesson, but it's the best lesson.

He is an arsonist. He wants to stand and watch people burn down. To push them to the point of anger or retreat.

I learned the best response, in this case and others, is to disengage. Recognize that the arsonist is looking for a reaction, a cross look, an unkind word, or perhaps a retreat. The arsonist wants to light the fire and watch it consume you.

What I am suggesting is not easy, it takes practice, it takes patience and it takes guts. You must not react or respond as the arsonist will try everything they have to ignite the fuse in you. Don't let them.

This is where my mindfulness techniques have saved me.

Breathe. Go back to yourself. Find that spot of no self for a few seconds. Be in control of you. Don't hand the power over, especially to someone you really don't value. The arsonist finds glee in the fire he is setting and your reaction is the oxygen. Deny him the oxygen. Suffocate the arsonist.

It will take time but eventually it will stop. The arsonist will realize you are not chasing the arsonist; instead, you are in control, you are putting out the fire burning inside you. You are in control.

We all want to defend ourselves, to say we are right and just. At some point, you just have to know you are right and just.

I have forgiven this brother for these attacks on me. In doing so, I refuse to give him power over me. I refuse to carry that weight.

In this age of social media, we have ample opportunities to engage with arsonists. Don't do it. Fortunately, on most social media platforms there is an "unfollow" or "unfriend" setting. Cell phones can block texts and calls. Use it.

Not chasing the arsonist is one the most valuable lessons I have learned. I finally significantly limited my interactions with my brother. I did not need the embers of his anger and vitriol he was sending to me. I am better for it. I am happier and I am at peace with my decision. My only regret is that I wish I had done it sooner.

Time to reflect: Think of all of the arsonist people in your life, the ones who take and never add. Forgive them and then block them. Let go and move on.

"No mud no lotus"
~ Thich Nhat Hahn

It's the muck that makes us value the flower. The flower doesn't exist without the muck. The rose doesn't exist without the manure.

In order to really enjoy the warmth, we must experience the cold. To know joy we must endure despair. To really appreciate a loved one we must know the sadness that goes with losing someone.

We often take things and life for granted. We don't consider the air we breathe until we are struggling for breath. We don't value clean drinking water until we hear stories about Flint, Michigan or wells that are contaminated with fracking waste.

Practicing Stoics believe in challenging yourself daily. To endure the muck of life everyday. It can be a physical challenge, a mental challenge, or in some cases, both. For those new to Stoicism, it's not an emotionless state; instead it's a practice of accepting things as they are and not buying into a victim mentality. Wishing or hoping things were different is fruitless.

I consider Stoicism to be Buddhism with an edge.

Stoics believe that the challenges we face make us appreciate the little things more. The more I read about Stoicism the more I bought into the daily challenge part. It can be as simple as intentionally fasting for a day to feel what it really means to be hungry. You may choose to keep your car windows down on a particularly cold day to really understand how much we value warmth.

I adopted a couple of Stoic practices. The first one was on a particularly hot and humid day in July. I intentionally turned the heat in my car to max heat and kept the windows shut. My goal was to gain a better appreciation of what it feels like to be cool. I drove for about 45 minutes, and within minutes I was sweating. I eventually arrived at my in-laws' house to pick up my daughter.

Upon exiting the car I immediately felt relief. Although humid outside, it was not the blistering heat of the car. When I entered the house, I immediately felt the refreshing coolness of the air conditioned room and an immediate appreciation of cool air.

When my daughter got in the car, she asked, "Why are the seats so hot and why is the dash burning?" It was a great opportunity to talk about Stoicism and the virtue of not taking anything for granted. She was not buying it. Oh well.

No mud, no lotus.

Another activity I do daily is a 30-second cold shower. Besides the health benefits that go along with cold showers (immunity boost, mental health improvements), you quickly know the value of warm water and comfort.

Another choice I've made is to take my dog outside for a walk without a coat. I do this every day, all year long. I also do not wear a coat when I go to work. And I stand on the porch barefoot while my dog takes care of his business.

The cold mornings and windy snowy days of November through April are enough to remind one how valuable socks, shoes and coats are.

These activities remind me of the material items that make us comfortable and that we take for granted. These activities, although very minor in scale, also serve as a great empathy reminder. Not every person has running water, let alone a hot shower. People struggle with clothing insecurity and my no-shoe mornings and no-coat days remind me of that. Empathy is not the same as compassion. Most people have a level of compassion but few people have empathy. Empathy is the ability to feel someone or something else's fear and/or pain.

I have far more empathy toward economic hardship having lived through the economic limitations placed on our family when my dad lost his business.

One of the pieces I have my students read is Plato's Cave. If you have not read it, I highly recommend it.

In it, Plato challenges us to not accept things as they are or to become complacent in our approach to life, eating the same things, only talking with the same people. He likens this to being chained in a cave where ignorance is truly bliss.

Learning only comes through struggle. We gain value in our lives by doing new things and accepting challenges: learning a new language, taking up photography, going to college.

No mud, no lotus.

In a response to The Cave, one of my students compared taking on new challenges and stepping out of her comfort zone to wearing uncomfortable shoes. She determined that she was going to metaphorically wear uncomfortable shoes at least once a week to challenge herself and, in some small way, peek outside her cave.

Compassion and empathy are at the heart of both Buddhism and Stoicism. You cannot have compassion until you have tasted what it means to wallow in the muck. You cannot appreciate the beauty in your life until you have suffered the ugliness society has to offer.

Break your chains that hold you in your cave and find a challenge everyday that will push you to be better and more compassionate.

Sometimes it's the smallest act that will make the biggest impact.

No mud, no lotus.

Time to reflect: Do something out of your comfort zone: sing karaoke, try out for community theatre or the school play, fast, take a cold shower. As my student said, "wear uncomfortable shoes."

"Sorry seems to be the hardest word"
~Sir Elton John

We all travel through life doing our best to avoid mistakes or messing up. I am not talking about turning left when you should have gone right. I am talking about real screw ups and the immediate reaction we normally have when we're called out, or our own reaction when we recognize we have done something wrong.

If you are like me, the response is usually immediate: "How do I get out of this mess, save face, and appear to be in control?" My immediate response is to look for ways to shield myself from the fallout so I blame others, lash out, do the old "it really is not that bad," deny, or in extreme cases go on the offensive.

It doesn't have to be this way. These reactions tend to push people away and inflame the situation. We don't like being told we are wrong or that we messed up. I suggest that when these situations occur, and they will, to take a second, find your breath, breathe in and out, push back against the immediate instinctual response and say instead: "I am sorry, I was wrong, my bad." Own it.

Apologies are underrated. Say you are sorry. It's really that simple. Too many people wander through their lives acting like a wrecking ball giving no thought to, or worse, not caring about the damage they have done or the havoc they have wreaked.

In our society, apologies are viewed as a sign of weakness when in reality they are a hallmark of strength, self reflection, and an ability to take ownership of our actions.

When I was a junior in high school, I had a brand new young English teacher, Mrs. Palmer. She was very nice, kind and thoughtful. She did all she could to keep a bunch of obnoxious 17-year-olds engaged in learning. She worked hard at her teaching and we rewarded her by being horrible.

Unfortunately for her, we learned early on that she was crier. So it became our goal to see if we could get her to cry. I am embarrassed to recount this as I am now a teacher.

There were several classes when my friends and I would intentionally try to make her cry. We did silly things like turning our desks around and facing away from the class. We said crazy things in response to her questions. We would call her by her first name. Once in the spring, several of us got up and watched the gym classes below out the window. No matter how much she implored us, we would not listen.

She cried.

The worst part for me was I knew what I was doing was wrong but did it anyway.

How this teacher did not throw us out of class is a credit to her drive and desire to teach us. What she was doing was important. I was fortunate. Had I been thrown out of her class (and on several occasions should have been), the cost/punishment at home would have been huge.

I do remember several of the books we read and discussions we had. She was good at her craft. I was terrible. We were terrible. But because of her and in spite of our push-back and shenanigans, I did very well on the final year-end New York State Regents exam. All credit goes to her.

Several years later, while visiting my parents, I ran into her and a few other former teachers at a local restaurant. By this time I had been teaching several years. I saw her and went to their table. I introduced myself and told her that I was now a teacher. I thanked her for what she did and told her I remembered her class with fondness. I also apologized for all of my immature idiocy. I told her that, now as a teacher myself, I was in awe of how she would not quit on us. No matter how bad we were, she did not quit and continued working to teach us.

She was gracious and laughed about what I recounted, simply saying, "You were a kid, it was OK." She added that those experiences made her a better teacher and she knew we were not malicious; "You were just being silly," she said.

So Mrs. Palmer, thank you for not quitting on me and the rest of us knuckleheads. And once again, I am sorry. I have either consciously or subconsciously adopted your easy going approach to teaching and learning.

There is never a wrong time to apologize. Always take the opportunity to own your mistakes. It matters.

Parents spend a great deal of time with their children teaching them how to take responsibility for their actions, asking them to apologize when they have made a mistake, pointing out the harm their words and actions can have. In a split-second those same parents can completely blow that out of the water by reacting with anger and accusations when they are wrong.

Our nation faces great discord, especially with regard to law enforcement and communities of color. Too many people of color are killed by law enforcement for minor traffic infractions or even just sleeping in their own bed, as examples. We all know the stories and they are unfortunately becoming far too common. Imagine if one of the officers involved in one of these deaths were to publicly apologize. I am not saying they would be admitting guilt, that is for the courts, but what if they were just willing to say, "I am sorry?"

While this can never bring back the loss of human life, it can go a long way in beginning to heal the deadly rift in our society. It's a beginning. Our society could benefit greatly from an emphasis on owning our actions, recognizing that we have wronged someone in some form, either word or deed, and simply apologizing. We all want to build strong, positive, healthy relationships and can start by owning our actions and recognizing and admitting when we are wrong.

On the flip side, for far less serious infractions we all may benefit from beginning with the idea that although that person did in fact harm us in some way, it was probably not intentional.

The next time someone cuts you off in traffic, bumps into you, or says something unkind, make an intentional choice. Instead of lashing out and allowing it to escalate, take a second, take a breath, breathe in and out and ask yourself, "Do I believe this person intentionally tried to harm me?"

The short answer is most likely no.

By apologizing, you own your actions and overtly show contrition. You are now the one with power and now it's the person who you offended or harmed who has the responsibility to either accept or reject. But your part is done.

You are not responsible for how they will react, so forgive yourself and vow to not make that same mistake again (although recognize you most likely will, and that it's OK as long as it was not intentional).

Time to reflect: This may be the most difficult yet: Apologize to someone you have wronged. You know you have done it. Go ahead. Don't text. Call them or meet face to face. In our "hide behind our computer screen or phone world," the ability to communicate genuinely and honestly is diminished. Face-to-face, or at minimum, voice-to-voice has a far greater impact and carries more weight.

Maybe you aren't that good
Really, maybe you aren't

We all want to think we are "that good," when in reality we aren't. It is a battle of the ego and reality. In our ego's need to be fed, it lies to us. We often look for reasons as to why we don't succeed. "It can't possibly can't be me." Instead we say things like:

"The teacher doesn't like me."
"They gave the job to someone less deserving."
"I really did not want it anyway."

Insert your reason why you did not succeed here: _____.

When we place blame on others we fail to take ownership of our own actions.

It may be true that there are some strikes against you. In reality, if you take stock of yourself, you simply may not be that good and it's OK.

We sometimes succeed or advance not through our achievement, but by whom we know. It's not our work ethic that determines our achievement, it's the unseen connection that opens the door to our future opportunities. As you reflect on your achievements, keep in mind that in some cases, we are not that good.

Sometimes it's good that we fail. That we fell flat and everyone saw it. Failure provides us the opportunity to get better, to become "that good." Growth only comes through failure and challenges.

"The obstacle is the way" is at the heart of Stoicism. This maxim posits that it's the challenges in life that provide the best opportunities to grow, get stronger, be more creative, and seek a new way. Self-reflection is one of the hardest things a person can do, but may also be one of the most valuable. Hard questions and challenges make us better. Do you ask yourself, "Did I really do all I could to succeed?" or do you say "She never liked me and gave me a bad grade."

I hear this all the time in school: "Mr. So-and-So is a jerk; he is a terrible teacher...." The grievances go on and on. But instead of blaming others for your under achievement, simply and honestly ask yourself: Did I spend enough time preparing for the exam or writing the paper? Did I proofread? Did I read the assigned articles?

I had these very conversations with my daughters in their studies. I had the same conversations with myself when I returned to college after my military service. It was the recognition that maybe I was not that good that pushed me to be good, or to at least be honest in my shortcomings.

I have 32 years of teaching experience and everyday on my half hour commute home, I replay the day. What went well, what did not go well, and how do I fix it? There have been days when I go to school the next day and apologize for the previous day's class. I knew that my teaching was "Not that good" and vowed to be better.

Don't be quick to blame others for your failures. It's OK to say you honestly gave it all you had and still came up short, maybe you are not that good and it's OK. But you can be.

Time to reflect: Write down three times you failed at something and honestly explain why.

Maybe you are wrong
The ego is the enemy

Battle stations, battle stations!! Shields up, armor on and sword drawn. Game on! It's an argument and you are right, you must win. There is nothing that can deter you, no throat you won't step on, no logical fallacy you won't use, no misdirection or sleight of hand you won't employ. You are right and you will win.

We all have been there, desperately wanting to show that bastard that our thoughts, that our knowledge is superior. Finally we will show him we are of superior intellect, perhaps at any or all costs.

But..... What if we are wrong?

I submit that if winning at all costs is your MO, you already lost.

In Stoicism, "the ego is the enemy" is not just a thought, it's a statement of fact. In our desire to be right, we may sacrifice really important things such as a friendship, our children, our parents, our marriage. To what end? Really think about that. To what end?

I am not talking about disagreements over whether to get the lifesaving surgery kind of stuff. That's obvious. Do that. Get the surgery.

I am talking about the little things, the trivial things that we will, in some cases, come to blows over. And once again to what end? Is being right about the name of the family dog from 40 years ago, was it Spot or Sparky, really that important?

We spend our time fighting and arguing over minor things in our quest to be right, when in reality it doesn't matter.

When you must win or be "right" at all costs, you are no longer rational or in control; the ego has seized you. There is no "fight or flight;" it's only fight. The ego needs to be validated. It needs to be fed and what feeds the ego is a win, no matter what.

The ego will push you to act irrationally; to lie, deceive and, in some cases, destroy to get what it needs, like an arsonist. The trick is to identify what is occurring and to disengage, to step back, to evaluate and determine whether this argument, this desire to be right is worth the damage it will inflict.

In 2010, an Internet meme made its rounds, outright lying about undocumented workers' access to Social Security. My mom emailed it to me and asked if it were true. My brother sent it to her. I knew it was not true and provided her evidence of the lies. I replied all to the email and hit send.

Within seconds came the attacks from my brother.

How dare I embarrass him by providing facts to refute his lie? Who did I think I was replying all? His boss was in that email.

I responded and asked if he was embarrassed because he propagated a lie or because the lie was exposed. The email strand grew lengthy and members of his family joined in on the assault. I continued my "reply all" responses to feed my ego. I knew no good would come from it, but that did not stop me. I had to win.

What could have been an opportunity to set the record straight and perhaps enlighten this person was lost.

In retrospect, I should not have replied at all. I should have simply replied to my mom and then privately sent an email to this brother pointing out the lie. Then it would have been on him to either correct it or continue it.

In my desire to be right I wreaked some serious havoc. I own that. But there it was, two ego-driven adults arguing over an Internet meme that did not matter.

We all want to be right all the time. We want to think that our thoughts, our way of doing things, our beliefs, our friends, our… is always right.

Take a second right now and think about your "wins," and how you've known you are right. Think about what happens if you eventually find out you were wrong. Do you accept that you were wrong? Maybe more importantly, what do you do when you accept you were wrong? Was the win worth the costs?

We are all wrong at some point. Hell, I live in that world. As a husband of a brilliant wife and father of two highly intelligent young adults, I find myself humbled quite frequently. I have learned that is OK.

Admitting you are wrong is one the most mature actions a person can take. It's an admission that, for whatever reason, you were mistaken. That's all. Somehow, though, in our society today, admitting you are wrong is somehow viewed as a sign of weakness, something that makes us less. I submit that admitting our mistakes and our wrong-headed way of thinking is an act of strength, courage and respect. It's a chance for a person, either privately in personal matters or publicly in public matters to clear the air, set the record straight, and accept what is known as fact.

Strength, courage and respect are hallmarks of a mature individual and society. By accepting your wrongness, you say to those listening, "I get it and respect you enough to tell you the truth."

Take a minute and consider how much less strife and consternation we would endure if we, all of us, could simply admit when we're wrong. Start right now. We all have to be holding onto something we know is wrong, whether it be a lie someone told us, a lie you perpetuated, cross words you uttered out of anger or worse. Whatever. Pick up your phone and call or text, get in your car or walk to whomever you know you treated wrongly and admit it. Apologize, admit you were wrong and move on.

I believe accepting responsibility and acting to rectify it is one of the many ways we can begin again to connect us to each other and heal the damage done. Recognizing you are wrong is the first step. Making amends for your actions is the second step. Vowing to be better is the third.

But like most things, we will mess up again and perhaps engage in some egoic "win-at-all-costs" behavior. For now though, recognizing that it's the ego calling the shot may help us take that breath and count to five or whatever is needed to slow us down. Do it before you lose something far more important than your temper.

Sun Tzu says, "Admitting you don't know is the beginning of wisdom." He is correct.

I say admitting you are wrong is the beginning of compassion and humanity.

Time to reflect: Like the apology homework, this one is tough. Contact someone you know you wronged, or were too hard-headed to admit you were wrong, and tell them you were wrong. Apologize.

Don't keep score
You will always lose

GOOOOOAAAALLLLLL!!!, a Hat Trick, Up by 4 in the bottom of the ninth, 27 - 3 with 32 seconds left, this game is over!, An ace, what a serve....

Keeping score makes sense in games. We keep score in Scrabble tournaments and Monopoly. The score determines which team or person wins because they have more points. We apply the same to our elections; normally the person with the most votes (points) wins. But then there's this thing called the Electoral College.... That is for a different book.

Keeping score in games is pretty basic stuff. Get the most points, win. That is for games, not life.

At the end of the day
Did you give more than you tay-ke

Measure life with that scale
And you will never fail

Give more than you take
That is a good cake to bake

You can add so much value
By giving more too

So do all you can
To make giving your plan

Have a beauty day

Love you both give em hell

In life we should NOT keep score. We should not approach life as a win-lose proposition. If winning is your approach, you may find yourself playing a lot of solitaire.

Many of us live our lives looking for ways to get even or to one-up each other. Someone tells a story, and immediately another person says, "that is nothing, let me tell you about…"

Another person makes us mad so we look for a way to get even. The only thing that happens in this scenario is a race to see who can do the worst thing, hopefully without breaking a law. No good comes from getting even, one upping, or keeping score in life.

In my life, in most cases, I've been successful in not approaching life as a win-lose proposition. I can only think of two situations, one in my personal life and one in my professional life, that I believe I have a score to settle.

At the same time, though, I know there is no way to even the score. I also know these situations are limiting me, holding me back from being completely at peace. My Stoic friends would say, "Let go, there is no getting even." My Buddhist friends would say, "Let go or be dragged." My friends are right.

Getting even or settling a score is miserable. It is akin to allowing the poison of anger and hatred to live in us and course through our veins. We spend time ruminating on how we were wronged and plotting and planning a way to get even. It is wasted time that we will never get back, time that can be used far more productively.

In your professional life keeping score limits your growth. If your goal is to always get even, you will lose focus on what is important: building your career not chasing someone else's.

In your personal life, keeping score can destroy your relationships. If you keep score on how often your partner or child does something you do not like, you are living transactionally.

The best and strongest relationships are transformational.

Consider why you are in the relationship. If it is to get ahead or achieve some personal gain, that is not a relationship, it is a business arrangement. You are looking for ROI (Return on Investment).

Not keeping score allows you to grow. Not keeping score forces you to reflect on WHY you are in the relationship. You build relationships by building; doing things because they need to be done.

One of the things I learned through many years of marriage and, quite basically, just living, is to expect nothing. I don't mean this in a negative way. Do the dishes not to score points, but because the dishes need to be washed. Fold the laundry, mow the lawn, wash the car because these jobs need to be done and you can do them. If you are keeping a scorecard in your head of all the things you have done, you are completely missing all the things your partner has done. Your score card is wrong. The score in your head is wrong.

So see a problem and solve a problem. Think of the little jobs you do as bricks in a strong foundation.

We all have things that bother us about our family members. It could be the clothes they left on the floor or the dishes left in the living room.

But even more concerning and dangerous than keeping score on household chores is what happens when we keep score on more personal issues like emotional slights or feelings of being unappreciated, disrespected, untrusted or worse. This is when not keeping score becomes difficult. We want to get out the scorecard, tally up the points, and put it in our pocket to use against this person later, when the time is just right to let them have it.

Unfortunately, the time we've been saving these points for is usually when we are ready to explode. And we will pull out our scorecard and read it like the Festivus "Airing of the Grievances." The points we are using become the tips of the darts we are throwing at the ones we profess to love.

Do not do this. Instead of tallying up points, take some time, put your thoughts into words, and share your feelings with those you feel have harmed you. Do not let it build; those points you have been tallying are a mirage.

They are not points, they are weapons.

Life can't be win-lose. If you play life like a game, especially in your personal life, you will lose.

Time to reflect:
If you are keeping score, STOP. Take the scorecard and tear it up. If you aren't keeping score, well done.

What is the worst that can happen?

"The obstacle is the way"   ~*Marcus Aurelius*

Before we really get into things here, I want to be clear. This chapter is about fear—the self-induced kind—and how debilitating it can be. This is not about the kind of fear that has you asking, "Is there someone in the house?" or "Will I get stabbed when I go through that door?" That is downright scary stuff right there. And yeah, that fear makes sense. Be scared.

Life is short
Grab all you can I exhort

Do not sit by idle
Be orderly not wild

People will not come to you'
You need to make it happen too

It is up to you
You have to

No complaining if you are sitting it out
Life is yours to live no doubt

If we wait for others to come to us
It will be a long while, like waiting for a bus

So get up and make it happen, Cap'n

Have a beauty day

Love you both give em hell

Self-induced fear is something we all experience. It's the stuff that paralyzes us and stops us from taking a chance or stepping outside of our comfort zones in order to embrace something or someone. The number of times I didn't do something only out of fear is many.

I love baseball. I was pretty good and yet when given the opportunity to try out for a team, I passed. I found every reason not to. I used the old, "Well the coach did not like my brother so he won't like me" and I did not try out.

The problem with buying into the fear of failure is that we will never know just how good we may have been. I am not naive enough to believe my high school baseball career would propel me to the Yankees (if the Yankee coaches are reading this now, I am available, call me), but I will never know what I passed up or what opportunities never materialized because of my fear. I will never know just how good I may have been.

As I reflected over time, I realized my fear was not grounded in thoughts of failure of making the team; I could have made the team. Instead, my fear festered in worries about failure that would happen once I did make the team.

"What if I strike out with the bases loaded in the bottom of the ninth?"
"What if I drop the double play ball at second base?"
"What if I get picked off stealing third base?"

All of those scenarios flashed through my brain and all of those things in baseball are likely to happen.

Professional baseball players make those mistakes all the time and they show up the next day and do it all again. And they get paid obscene amounts of money. In baseball if you are successful 30% of the time at the plate, you will make 15 million dollars a year.

Get this. You can fail 70% of the time and still be rich. Weird.

Overcoming the "what ifs" is difficult and, for many, it stops us in our tracks. We create all sorts of reasons NOT to do something.

I suggest that instead of thinking: "What if I ...", instead try, "What is the worst that can happen?"

If it's a team you are considering trying out for, do it. What is the worst that can happen? If you don't make it, so what? You are already not on the team. If it's a college you are considering, apply. What is the worst that can happen? You are already not going to school there, so nothing will be different. But if you apply, you may get accepted. If it's a new skill you'd like to try like art, music, painting, rock climbing, fly fishing, improv etc... What is the worst that can happen?

A few years ago, I had a young woman in class, Kristin, and like all my students I asked her many questions to get to know her better. I asked her what her hobbies were or what she did for fun. She responded that she was on the golf team and I said that was great. I asked if she was good and she responded, "not very, but it is fun" and then she added "how can I learn and get better if I don't play?"

As the year progressed she would regale me with her new exploits. She signed up for the talent show and played guitar and sang in front of a couple hundred people; she had never performed in front of anyone. She played basketball and rugby, she wrote and performed stand up. Her list of activities was endless. She lived the "What is the worst that can happen?" life.

Her life is more full and rich because she doesn't let fear of failure or success limit what she will do.

I learned a lot from Kristin. Writing this book is one of those things. This book has been kicking around for a couple of years now and I finally took the leap and sent it to a publisher and they accepted it.

Dabbling with painting, jewelry making, and woodworking are other things I was inspired to try. I learned from Kristin that if the painting flops, there is more paint. If the copper snaps, there is more copper. And if I cut the board too short there is more wood.

In life you don't need to swing at every pitch, but you will miss every pitch you don't swing at.

You will fail, you will make mistakes, but how else will you grow? Live "The Obstacle is the way."

For Kristin, I know it's only a matter of time until I turn on HBO and she has her own stand up special. She is that good, primarily because she doesn't let fear stop her. Maybe you are that good. Try. What is the worst that can happen?

Time to reflect: Finally do the thing you have always wanted to do. Learn the piano or guitar. Join the choir, make a film, do improv. Take an art class, finish high school or college or your masters or your Ph.D. Whatever it is, do it. What is the worst that can happen?

*Update: As this book was being finalized, I bumped into Kristin. That is her real name, she gave me permission to use it. She was leaving the next day to go to NYC to give the music scene a try. She has a band, Women's National Hockey League, they are good. No fear. She sees every opportunity to live life.

"It's not personal, it's not business"

"Don't bite the hook" ~ *Pema Chodron*

"Watch out! He is over the line, what a jerk!"

"Why is he following so closely? I'll fix him!" And then you give him the brake lights and the one finger salute.

"Owww, be careful, you are so clumsy!"

All of us have heard these statements or maybe even said them. These are the minor transgressions that set us off. The inadvertent actions that may darken our mood and actions for the next few minutes or even longer.

If we allow it.

While the incident may be minor in scale, we magnify it. We wonder: How could that person be so careless or thoughtless? How can they do that to me? We play it out over and over in our head, and then we talk about and relive the experience when we get to work or school.

You bit the hook. Can you feel the hook pulling you away from where you want to be to the place this minor incident takes you? You bit the hook and that hook now controls you.

What we neglect to recall is that sometimes we make these same careless or thoughtless mistakes. We cut off people when we drive, we snap at a friend. I call it, "caught in the act of being human." Rarely have I met a person who intentionally meant to harm others; the arsonist is the exception.

- Note: the distinction between these examples and the arsonist example is intent. Biting the hook can be the precursor to chasing the arsonist. Ignore the hook and there is no arson. Life is good.

Of all the practices for sane living, this one may be the most difficult to master—largely because our immediate response is to react and defend—but at the same time, learning to overcome it may provide the most rewards. Reaction tends to be immediate and angry; defending often means going on the offensive.

Baseball metaphor:
You don't need to swing at every pitch. Some pitches are up and away, some are down and in. Others are in the dirt. While some pitches may fool you, the ones in the dirt are the ones you need to lay off.

The thing that separates the top tier hitters and the next level is plate discipline. The best hitters sometimes have 15/20 vision. They see the 97 MPH fastball, they see the seams of the curve ball and they see the slider breaking down in that fraction of a second.

The best people have the best "people discipline." They swing only when they need to and rarely at a pitch in the dirt.

Biting the hook is like swinging at a pitch in the dirt. You aren't going to hit it, you are going to look foolish and the other players will laugh at you as you head back to the dugout.

To overcome this we must learn to take a second or five, breathe in and out, before responding. Think of the coworker that snaps at you for no good reason, or your child that lashes out at you and you don't know why. Taking the time to recognize that the anger directed at you is most likely not because of you. You are only the recipient. Do not react.

Don't bite this hook or swing at that pitch. Now is your chance to be a friend. The person who snapped at you is normally kind and pleasant so something must be amiss. Now is your chance to use humor or kindness to disarm and de-escalate instead of putting on your armor and waging war or engaging in a small skirmish that leaves hurt feelings.

As a friend, your goal is to limit the damage the hook is doing; look for a way to help them to get unhooked.

We need to learn to give people an out, a way to save face when they have dropped their line. We do that by not biting, but by seeking understanding, giving grace through generosity of our human spirit. This approach is meant to seek understanding first.

Not biting the hook is something I struggle to overcome. I have made some improvements, but I'm still not where I want to be. Like most of us, though, I have plenty of opportunities to practice because I take every transgression as a personal attack, when in reality they are not. In many cases, I believe, the person drawing our ire may not even recognize that what they did or said caused us anguish.

Recently I was shopping and headed to the checkout. In all honesty, I did not recognize any sort of line and simply started unloading my goods as the person ahead of me was leaving the lane. I heard a very loud and frustrated "Really?" coming from behind, I quickly looked over my shoulder and saw a young woman with an exasperated look and could hear her eye roll. I bit the hook. "Yes, really," I replied, and continued to put my stuff on the counter.

Here it was, I bit. I knew it almost immediately. I missed an opportunity to practice what I preach. In that second, instead of continuing on in a self-righteous way, I should have apologized and said, "I am sorry, I did not know there was a line. Please go ahead."

For me, the good news is that I did recognize my insensitivity. I could have taken the next step and apologized for my rude and disrespectful retort after finishing my checkout, but instead, I simply took my own "man I screwed up" as penance enough, though really it was not.

Instead of de-escalating and disarming, I perpetuated and probably made that young woman feel poorly for at least a few more minutes.

So, to that young woman at Sam's Club, I am sorry for being insensitive. I was wrong. Because of that simple interaction, I am now more aware, and that is something.

"The people you will meet today will be ungrateful
and mean and short sighted and frustrating"
Marcus Aurelius

While the Aurelius quote is true, it doesn't mean you must be ungrateful, mean, shortsighted, and cause others to be frustrated. You don't need to buy into the ugliness.

While we cannot control the speed of the wind that blows our sails, we can control the direction it pushes us.

I live in a rural area. The road that goes through the village is notorious for having slow drivers, and for good reason. For many years I would rail against them, shouting, "Come on, let's go!" (Among various other unkind things.) Sometimes I allowed my frustration to transgress into anger. By the time I arrived home, the anger had subsided but the feelings of frustration were still present, and for the next ten minutes I would share my frustration with anyone willing to listen; sometimes whoever was present was forced into an unwilling listener role.

I was able to overcome this by simply thinking of that slow driver as my mom. Would I yell at my mom? No.

Now, when this slow driving situation happens (at least weekly), I sit back and enjoy the drive. It's amazing the beautiful things you find when we learn to slow down and not react. Enjoy the drive.

Time to reflect: The next time you find yourself in a situation where someone commits a minor infraction against you, bumps you, follows too closely, or drives too slowly, take a breath and remind yourself that you also make mistakes. That person got caught in the act of being human and made a mistake. Your reflection could be as simple as taking a few seconds to ask yourself, "Was that intentional?" It probably was not. Let go or be dragged.

People are weather

A bit of rain
No pain

Weather we can't control
So sit down and eat an ice cream bowl

Do one thing for someone
Laugh and make it fun

Leave things better than you found
Get up and move around

Fold towels or do laundry
Do more than exist or just be

Have a beauty day

Love you both, give em hell

My daughter used to speak of a young man in her classes who was perpetually pretty erratic. I asked her once why she did not talk to him, to show some compassion. Be a friend.

She responded, "I am not lighting that wildfire." I got it.

As we get older we begin to see that some of the people we know are either a perpetual tornado, rain cloud, or ray of sun. I am not talking about a one off, that one time someone you know to be consistently positive, who one day is not their usual self. In that case, it is time to be a friend and see how you can help.

I am talking about the people whose personality or MO is consistently tornadic, cloudy with a good chance of rain or perpetually sunny.

Worst case is the tornado. That's the guy who consistently shows up and in 15 seconds has either figuratively or literally dismantled or undone much of what you were doing. It may have been through unkind words or even acts, but he does it every time.

On the flip side is the person who shows up and is like a ray of sunshine in your life.

There is a teacher and a former assistant I work with and every time we speak they make me better. The pick me up is not necessarily what they say, instead it's their attitude and genuine kindness. I do my best to meet up with them a couple times a week, usually it's just in passing, and every time we part I am reinvigorated.

They are a ray of sunshine.

As for the rain clouds, we all know them—the ones who come in everyday, and complain. They rarely see what could be, instead focusing on what was and why it was bad. They are the worriers, the "What if..." people who intentionally or unintentionally put a damper on your day... if you let them.

In Stoicism, Marcus Aurelius encourages us to prepare for those weather factors. If you have a meeting with Tom and Tom is a tornado, be prepared. Expect Tom to be a tornado, expect him to try to wreak havoc, wreck you and your day. Be on guard and when the conversation begins. Don't expect him to be anything less than the weather factor—the tornado—he is.

Perhaps Tom Tornado will surprise you and instead of showing up as a tornado, he'll just be a strong wind. That is a win.

When you see Randy Rain Cloud coming, know he is a rain cloud. Don't expect Randy Rain Cloud to be anything else and prepare yourself for the drizzle or even downpour that may accompany him.

We cannot expect people to be anything other than what they are.

As for the rays of sun, those are the good ones, the ones that brighten your day, energize, encourage, and uplift. Seek those people and surround yourself with them.

Dealing with the weather can be frustrating but if we prepare for it, it may not be so bad. We take an umbrella when it rains or wear a warm coat when it's cold, and we find the tools that will help deflect some of the damage the tornado or rain cloud will do. Keep your interactions short and to the point and move on to better weather.

The good news is Tom Tornado eventually blows out and Randy Rain Cloud eventually runs out of rain and then the sun comes out. The people that dampen our spirits eventually go away and then Mary Lou or Kate, the rays of sunshine, shine brightly and the sky clears and life is good.

Surround yourself with sun rays, but be aware and prepared for bad weather. It's inevitable. How we respond is up to us.

Time to reflect: Make a list of the tornadoes, rain clouds and rays of sunshine. Do your best to spend as much time in the sun and limit your exposure to the tornadoes and rain clouds. I know it's not possible to completely ignore the storms, but always be prepared and don't expect them to be anything other than what they are. Always carry an umbrella.

Bend, don't break
This one is for all the parents

Our oldest daughter has always been a spirited soul. Wise beyond her years. In fact, our good friend Deb always referred to her as an "Old Soul." From the age of six she was involved in countless social awareness and social justice activities. She made many trips to Washington, DC to protest or meet with legislators pushing for more compassionate and humane policies in every arena. In 3rd grade she spearheaded a protest at her school over what she perceived to be an unfair lunch policy. This earned her a meeting with the principal. She took the petition she had several of her classmates sign. We were very proud of her.

Her first words were not mom and dad, but, "What's that?" and eventually, "Why?"

She was and still is fiercely independent, I can't count the number of times I heard, "I got it, I don't need your help."

I remember discussing this with our pediatrician and she smiled and said, "Bend, don't break."

The doctor encouraged us to recognize the maturity already present in her and to find a way to harness it, not destroy it, to help her develop her skills, not force her to fit a mold. She said the worst thing we might do is limit her independence. She was right.

Our oldest daughter had it mapped out from the age of 14: a fairly close state university for a BS in social work, and then onto an MSW and LSW.

She breezed through it, seemingly effortlessly, graduating early and finishing her MSW by the age of 23.

Our second daughter was, in my mind, a little less independent. She is more willing to play by the rules and not challenge them. She doesn't ask why. She accepts things for what they are.

I was wrong about her independence. I had presumed that she, being a true introvert, also meant she was less independent. I quickly learned, however, that one has little to do with the other. In fact, she did not attend her high school graduation because she was flying to London for a six week intensive summer study abroad program. As for college, she applied and was accepted at an international university in London, though she chose not to attend.

My thoughts of her as less independent were shredded.

This daughter is an artist in every sense of the word. If you know artists, they think differently, they see things we will never see. It's truly a gift. It took me a while to really understand this. Now that I know more about her way of seeing the world, I am in awe.

Her true passion is art and animation, and she is very good; but she is pragmatic enough to recognize how difficult a field it can be, especially for a woman. My wife and I encouraged her to follow her passion and to throw herself into the art/animation world.

She did. After a year at a state university she went all in, applying to the number one animation school in the world—literally the world. She did not get in. This setback did not stop her. She finished her studies at another state university. Before her now is a choice between graduate school or beginning her career.

As a teacher I hear many different worries from seniors, especially with their college struggles. Many are very excited to attend the local university while a good number, not so much.

Many of the students attend solely because their parents receive a discounted tuition, while others attend because they want to.

But it's another group that I feel for.

I had a student a few years ago who loved politics and history; she took every history/social studies course our school offers. She did an independent study with me to further delve into Nigeria as it moves through the developing stage.

In a casual conversation, I asked where she was attending university and if she was excited to study political science/international relations. She hung her head and said, "I have to go to Penn State." I responded that their political science/international relations program was excellent and very respected.

She then continued and with a sadness in her voice, "My parents won't let me study political science or international relations. They said those degrees are worthless and they demand that I study something in a field so I can easily get a job. If I don't, they will not pay for my college."

I asked her what she wanted to do and she replied, "To not go to Penn State but to definitely study political science in Vermont. I want to work for the State Department."

She ended up at Penn State and studied engineering.

Broken, not bent.

So, to my parent friends or those soon-to-be parents, tap into your children's interest, encourage them to explore and to follow their passions. Encouraging children and taking interest in their hobbies validates them. It makes for tremendous opportunities to connect, learn, encourage, and explore for both parents and kids. When it comes to our children, we must learn to guide, not drive; selectively sculpt, not force form; and most of all, to allow them to be who they are.

OK, one more story. Every semester I write my cell number on the board for all my students. I tell them it's for two reasons:

    1. The first is the academic things. I tell them to text me if they are going to be late, or if they have a question about class. Or in case

they're wondering if they should pick me up an iced coffee on the way to school? (Students actually do that.)

2. The second and, by far most important reason, is to let them know that I am available for a ride home, anytime, if they ever find themselves in a situation where they need help. No Questions Asked.

Their safety is the most important thing to me and it should be to you. I always tell them they should call their parent/guardian first, for obvious reasons including that parents and guardians will find out eventually. I am the backup.

Kids will make mistakes. It's important to remember that making mistakes is not a reason for disappointment, it's an opportunity to learn and to build trust, for both us and our kids.

My wife and I extended this same offer to our daughters:
"Call anytime, anywhere, and we will come get you. No Questions Asked."
I tell my students and my daughters to think of the alternative; they could find themselves in a hospital room or worse, all because they were worried about a phone call. And in all reality, parents will find out what you did anyway. Better to be safe than sorry and take an opportunity to build trust.

Time to reflect:
Hug your child. Love your children as THEY ARE, not how you want them to be. Let them grow and explore and make sense of the world. Know they will make mistakes, that they'll mess up. That is OK; we all did that. But if you deny them who they are, they may pull away from you, abandon your relationship, or worse. If they are afraid to ask for help, that is a bad place to be.

You didn't build it...

"We all sit at fires we did not build and drink from wells we did not dig."
Gwendolyn Brooks

We are standing on the shoulders of those who came before and some of them were giants.

My father was a Korean War vet. He was drafted when he was 21 to go 12,000 miles away to fight in a war he most likely did not understand.

He did it.

For his service he lost his hearing and lived with shrapnel in his hands nearly to the end of his life. Artillery barrages and .50 caliber machine gun fire can have those effects on a person.

He rarely spoke about his experiences, as is true for most combat veterans.

I was able to get him to discuss his sacrifice, not his experience.

Prior to being drafted into the ARMY, he was practicing with the Rochester Red Wings, a AAA affiliate of the St Louis Cardinals. By all accounts, he had a promising professional baseball career ahead of him as a catcher.

Near the end of his life I asked if he resented sacrificing his baseball career for two years in the ARMY. I thought for sure I would hear, "Man I missed my chance."

Instead, I was shocked with his very direct answer:

"No, when your nation calls on you to sacrifice, you answer."

That is sacrifice. And sacrifice is what "I built it" rejects.

It's almost illogical: "I built it." It's difficult for me to think of something more arrogant than the assertion that somehow a person's success was solely created by them. It's laughable. An obvious rejection of reality.

Plato, in his writing of The Cave, addresses this very idea.

Plato writes that people are most comfortable in their own surroundings and perceptions of them. They believe the meaning they derive is the only meaning. This is what it means to be in the cave. When people emerge from their caves, he writes, they begin to see the world as it really is, not the world they believed to be true. But to emerge from the cave is to confront the ignorance and hubris we harbor about the world and our role in creating and understanding it; this is a difficult step for many people to take.

He says this:

"He will then proceed to argue that this is
he who gives the season and the years,
and is the guardian of all that is in the visible world,
and in a certain way the cause of all things
which he and his fellows have been accustomed to behold?"

My contemporary interpretation:

Many of the things which allow us to succeed were created long before by someone else but we are unable or unwilling to admit it. Many of us believe ourselves to be solely responsible for our success without acknowledging those who laid the foundation to make our success possible.

Even 2500 years ago Plato pointed out no one builds anything alone. Plato shows us that we just pick up where others left off.

No one "builds it" on their own. To believe otherwise is to deny the sacrifice of millions who came before and those who sacrifice now.

If you attended college, it's most likely because your parents provided the resources, SAT review courses, and paid the taxes for a good high school. That foundation allowed you to advance. Even if you came from a family of limited financial resources, you probably had someone in your life who supported and encouraged you.

But it's not that simple. Most likely, your parents benefited in the same or similar manner as you. That is, those who came before them also laid a foundation, and so on.

Anyone claiming that they built their own business, discounts the public infrastructure laid to build the business, the roads, the bridges, the water, the sewers, telephone lines, creation of the Internet, etc. There is nothing wrong with building a business, but no one builds "it" on their own.

I learned that my success is built on the work and sacrifices of those who came before. We are able to live our lives without fear of invasion. Most of us don't think twice about running water or clean air. We live more freely and with greater opportunity because of the work of millions of others who came before as well as those working now to provide us with necessary resources.

I am a teacher only because my dad worked two jobs and my mom worked full-time while also instilling in me a love for learning. They showed me what hard work looks like.

Although my parents struggled financially, I really never went without.

When I was in 9th grade, Nikes were just becoming popular and I wanted them. My parents could only afford the "Winner" by Sears, and that was a stretch. But I was relentless. I had to have Nikes. And I got them.

I always wondered what my parents sacrificed so I could have Nikes. I spoke with my mom a few years ago and all she said was, "That is what parents do; they sacrifice for their kids." Recognizing the sacrifice of others for our wellbeing is what is completely missed by a person who believes "they built it."

Perhaps that is what is missing today in our country: shared sacrifice, a commitment to "build a fire" or "dig a well" for someone else.

Many other nations require a mandatory service to the nation, either in the military or some other form. I believe that would be a valuable lesson in shared sacrifice and recognition that no one makes it on their own.

You did not build it, you are standing on the shoulders of millions who came before: your great grandfather from Italy or Poland, your parents who bought Nikes. Just recognize that.

If you are a business owner and are writing out your quarterlies, recall that it's those taxes that provide the infrastructure people use to frequent your business.

If you are a young person reading this, ask who got you here and what were they willing to do to get you to this place in time?

If you participated in extracurricular activities that required early morning practices or late night rehearsals, think about who it was that got you up, drove you there, waited for you, cheered for you, consoled you, and paid for it all.

More importantly, consider what your sacrifice will be.

Your success is built not only on the sacrifice of others but also the blood of others.

Remember that millions have made the ultimate sacrifice for you to complain or claim you built a business. Recall those young men hitting the beaches at Sword and Omaha, those who landed at Inchon, in the Ia Drang, or Ramadi, Kabul or Fallujah. They sacrificed so you could build.

Time to reflect: Make a list of all the people who came before you to get you where you are today. A simple genealogical tree. Research who they were, and where they came from. What did they do before arriving here and what did they do when they arrived? Appreciate all their sacrifice. If they are still alive, call them and thank them. Lay the foundation for the next generation.

"Give love away"
~John Roberts

John Roberts, along with my wife, is the finest educator I know. I was his student teacher in 1990 in Avon, New York, a small upstate town. He was beloved as a teacher and coach not only because of his skill, but also for his practice of "Giving love away." In Sanskrit this practice is called Maitri.

From Yogapedia: Maitrī (Sanskrit; Pali: mettā) The term maitri can be translated from Sanskrit as "loving-kindness," "benevolence," or "friendliness." The concept is central to the Buddhist practice of loving-kindness.

Pema Chodron says it best: Unconditional friendliness.

John is the kind of guy who will do whatever it takes to help you succeed, not only through kindness and encouragement, but also by kicking you in the rear when needed. I have been on the receiving end of both. I subconsciously learned this practice from him. John was not an active practitioner of Buddhism. His practice was innate and genuine. He is a Buddha.

Those who practice Maitri do it because it's right. It's an "Action without adulation" way of life. If you do things to receive recognition or to get something in return, you are living a transactional life.

Maitri is a transformational way of life. Never withhold love. Give it freely with no precondition or expectation. Love isn't transactional, it's transformational.

John has officiated several weddings, and when I was asked to perform the marriage of two former students I could think of no better person to help me take on this awesome responsibility.

John told me he uses the theme of "Give love away" at each of the weddings for which he is the officiant. Those simple words made it all make sense. That is what a wedding is—a promise to give love unconditionally and forever, to ask nothing in return and, even on your worst day, to give love.

It was an honor to perform the wedding ceremony. I was speaking with the bride and groom prior to the ceremony and I saw "the look." It's the look only two people who truly were giving love can give. You know it when you see it.

As I mentioned earlier, everyday I text my daughters a small poem. My oldest always responds with a "Love you too." My youngest daughter says nothing. At first I was saddened by the non-response and I wondered, "Did she get it, did she read it?" It took me a while to learn that this should not be my concern.

Maitri is not about, "Did they get it?" The question is "Did I send it?" I was looking for validation; I was being transactional. Maitri is about the sending. Did you take the time to pass on a good thought, kind word, silly poem, or even something larger without expecting anything in return?

In Stoicism it's: Expect nothing.

Do I know my youngest daughter received it? Yes. Do I know she read it? No. And now, I am OK with that uncertainty. Perhaps I should be concerned when she begins replying.

Another thing I started doing during the pandemic was sending bracelets, necklaces, and other small tokens of appreciation to people I know and others I don't. I sent 30 or more bracelets to a former student, now a doctor in Brooklyn.

She and her team were on the front lines of the COVID war. She sent pictures of the doctors and nurses wearing the bracelets and necklaces as they were going into battle to save COVID patients.

On a personal note, I felt I had to do something; my mom died from this monster, and since I was not qualified in any medical field, at a minimum I knew I could send encouragement. My former student texted me and sheepishly asked if I could send more and that she would pay. I responded with more, and a stern but friendly warning to never ask to pay again. I would send her anything I had.

The day after my mom's death I received a video message from another student. She had recorded the Beatles "Let It Be" for me. This student and I often discussed our musical interests and she knew how much I loved this song. Her version is the best version I've heard, not because it is perfect but because she did it. Maitri.

I made and sent 15 or so bracelets to the nurse who stood down the anti-mask crowd in Arizona. More recently, when I see or hear a story about someone struggling with a tough situation or doing good in the world, I send a bracelet and a personal note. I expect nothing in return.

The St, Louis DA, Kim Gardner, comes to mind along with Steve Roth in Columbus, Ohio. Both of these warriors are taking on tough issues and keep showing up everyday. I was pleasantly surprised with a kind note from DA Gardner, but that was completely unexpected.

Maitri is all about giving, never about receiving. I believe those who are true practitioners of Maitri struggle with receiving; at least it feels that way to me.

Loving kindness is not just for others, it's also for you. I am learning to not be so hard on myself, to laugh more and fret less. To say thank you when a kind word is offered.

The first time I met my wife's grandfather we engaged in a conversation and I, with my self-deprecating sense of humor, said something unkind about myself. Her grandfather looked at me and said, "You know Andy, there are enough people out there in the world that will run you down with words and actions, you don't need to do it to yourself." That little pearl has stuck with me forever. Consistently practicing it is another story.

Time to reflect:
Today, right now, at this very minute, do something kind for someone. Send a text, walk up and give a hug, give love away and expect nothing in return. If you make Maitri part of your life practice, make it a habit, you will be better for it and so will the world.

Who is your "go to?"

Who is your flat-tire friend?

OK, so this is a secret all teachers have and are reluctant to share and may even deny: every teacher has a "go to" student. Some have favorites, but we all have a "go to."

It's the kid who may sit in the back, look bored out of her gourd, but can offer a mind blowing insight on Britain and its decision to leave the EU, or perhaps an evaluation on the Senate consideration to end the filibuster.

You know she knows, she knows you know she knows. It's kind of a game. But when it's crunch time and the teacher needs someone to push the other students, she is your "go to."

I remember many of my go to's: Lauren, Paulina, Scarlett, Samir, Rohit, Anup, Matt, Pat, Sondi, Sohayla, Willie, Billy. Many of whom I am now friends with.

In life we need "go to's." I call them "Flat-tire Friends."

We all need Flat-tire Friends.

You know the friend, whether it's 2PM or 2AM, they will show up and help you, no questions asked. Some of those "go to's" in my class are now Flat-tire Friends.

November 3, 2020

Be good today
Do what you can to lead the way

Hopefully we will right the ship
The last 4 a bad trip

Look for goodness in all
In any case stand TALL

People often act out of fear
Be the truth and be clear

No sitting around get in the game
If we wait for others we are lame

Have a beauty day

Love you both give em hell

When my mom died from COVID, I was wrecked. I spoke with her two to three times a day for the past several years, especially since my dad died.

When my sister called and shared that my mom was COVID positive, I knew it was game over. I knew without talking with my mom that she would refuse treatment. In reality, she was tired and I think because of her strong faith, she was ready to join my father and older sister. I called my mom and, as delicately as I could, discussed COVID. She was mentally sharp and said she would not take any treatment. We spoke about the end result of the most severe cases. She knew it and was prepared. I was not.

I received the diagnosis call on Wednesday and by the following Monday she was gone. I called her senior living community and spoke with a nursing supervisor and she held the phone to mom's ear on her last day, so I could tell her how much she meant to me. She knew, but I wanted her to hear this one more time. My biggest fear was that she would die alone.
After her death I spoke with the facility director and she assured me that a male nurse, one my mom thought very highly of was with her in the final minutes. I was relieved.

That is when the true Flat-tire Friends show themselves: When you are at your worst.

The news of my mom's death hit Facebook at about 6:30PM. Many emojis of love appeared along with loving words of compassion and remembrances of my mom. She was well-liked and well-known in her communities, both in the Rochester and Alexandria Bay areas. I was overwhelmed by the beautiful outpouring of love that flooded my page. It was real and it was genuine and it was beautiful.

The Flat-tire Friends phone calls:
As I was reading and responding to messages of love, my phone rang, it was Samir. The first Flat-tire Friend to call. We talked for a few minutes, said our goodbyes, and planned to meet after COVID.

Next was Deb. She is like a sister to me, full of love, grace and kindness.

She was followed by Matt, Rohit, then Anup. Patrick was next and then finally Willie.

My good friend in DC, Bill, did not get the news for a day or two, and then he called.

All who called expressed their regret and sadness and all said that if I needed anything, to call. They meant it. That is what a Flat-tire Friend is. They are the "go to," the one who will show up and sit with you on your worst day. They don't have to say a word. It's just about being there.

To have a Flat-tire Friend, you must be a Flat-tire Friend. You must be genuine, real, and compassionate. You must want to help even and especially on the other person's worst day. A true Flat-tire Friend lives Maitri.

Know your Yoda

We all need a Yoda. We all need those one or two people who will listen when we need an ear or give it to us straight when we need some advice. Your Yoda may or may not be the same as your Flat-tire Friend.

Sometimes we need that person who can be objective, someone who is close, but not too close to us. The person who will give it to us straight. The person who can look us in the eye and tell us we are wrong, for no other reason than the mutual respect we hold.

I have two.

For me, my wife is my first Yoda. We have an incredible relationship. After nearly 30 years, she can look at me or catch a tone in my voice and know I need some guidance. She is my Yoda.

Many years ago I was on a rant about teaching; complaining, grousing, finding fault. You name it, I complained about it.

I recall being particularly negative one day, and she had had enough. As I was leaving my office, she looked at me and said, "If teaching is such a drag on you, quit. Find another job." Her words stopped me cold.

She wasn't mean, she wasn't angry, she was matter of fact. And she was right.

I replied, "I don't want to quit."

She said, "Stop complaining."

I now check myself anytime I find myself veering into the negative zone.

My other Yoda is the guidance counselor/coach at my school. Matt is a guy that I can talk to about anything.

He has mastered, "Do you want an ear or do you want advice?" I am sure his counseling background has helped with that.

I believe it is just who he is.

Find your Yoda. Better yet, be a Yoda.

Time to reflect:
Text your Flat-tire Friends and tell them how much you appreciate them and that you are available to them at any time.

Your word is your bond
Baseball cards

Baseball cards cemented this one in my head.

My first real teaching job was as a summer school teacher at New York State Juvenile Justice Residential Facility in upstate New York: The Oatka Residential Facility. Another teacher and I were responsible for teaching basic math and English concepts to a group of 15 - 18 students. All convicted felons. I taught at this school during summer sessions for three years, 1990 - 1992. My experiences there taught me that the world may not always be a kind or fair place. This was not a holding facility, it was a prison with razor wire, gates, every door locked, and some very big YDAs (Youth Development Aides), aka guards.

Every resident was rated each day on their behavior, IR - Irresponsible, R - Responsible, and VR - Very Responsible.

An IR got you what we would consider "solitary": Immediately to your room (cell), and no time at night for television or phone calls. Food was served in your room. An R was average. A VR got you some extras, perhaps an extra half hour of TV or an extra call, or perhaps a food treat. I handed out mostly R and VR's. I can't think of a time when a student earned an IR. They were just kids.

The kids were 12 - 16, all felons convicted of crimes like robbery, armed robbery, drug dealing, and murder. This may sound odd, but they were some of the nicest kids I met. (I owe my continued teaching career to one student in particular, I will discuss that at the end.)

These kids were honest and very open in discussing why they were locked up. We had access to their files. I never read the files, instead I talked with my kids. I wanted to know them. You can't really know a person from a piece of paper. Papers are flat. Reading a file may teach you what they did but you can't know the "why" or who they are. You only get that face to face.

I was one of eight summer school teachers; there were four teams of two teachers. The teaching crew I worked with were the finest people I met. Good people first, good teachers second. Although I have no empirical data, I would say there is a correlation between good people and good teachers.

The other teacher on my team was Bob Shaffer who, fortunately for me, was another baseball fan.

Each team was assigned a different colored t-shirt. Bob and I were the green team.

I remember talking with one of my students, he was 12. This young man was about six feet tall and weighed no more than 125 pounds. I thought to myself, "What could this kind, funny, sweet kid do to be locked up in a place like this?"

I asked him why he was there and he shared that he robbed stores, then laughed and said he was not very good at it.

He was arrested while robbing a store. This particular time his friend was driving the scooter getaway vehicle, and it stalled as they were fleeing. The store owner pulled him off the back. The driver got away.

He told me he was convicted of armed robbery because he told the store employee he had a gun, although he told me he did not really have one.

I followed up with the obvious "Why?" and his answer exploded my world.

He was 12 and his mom was a crack addict. His father was non-existent and his 9-year-old sister needed to eat, so he robbed stores. I asked about his younger sister and where she was and all he said was, "I don't know."

I left it at that.

In that brief exchange, I questioned everything I had learned throughout my entire previous education. How could a 12-year-old be pushed to the point of robbing stores to feed his sister? If he was guilty, then we are guilty.

I thought about how this 12-year-old young man had seen and done things I would never know. Every adult responsible for him had failed him. I thought about him a lot on my 2.5 hour drive home. I cried. Yes, I drove 2.5 hours each way to teach. It was that valuable for me.

On that drive home, I wondered if, for many of the young men locked up at New York State Juvenile Justice Residential Facility, their actions were survival, not criminal. I still wonder what kind of society makes a 12-year-old rob a store to feed his sister. Perhaps he is a victim just as much as the store owner.

Since both Bob and I loved baseball, we used fantasy baseball statistics to teach basic math concepts. Everyday we would cut the box scores out of the newspaper, tape them together, make copies and hand the copies out. Old school fantasy baseball.

Each student drafted a team and they used basic math concepts to add up runs, hits, home runs, calculate ERA, BA, etc. The student whose team had the best stats for the week won a pack of baseball cards.

The Rochester Democrat and Chronicle did a story on our unorthodox approach to teaching basic math concepts and our individual card collecting.

My learning...

It was a Sunday night at about 11:45PM. I had to be up at 5AM and drive two and half hours, and it hit me:

I did not buy baseball cards for that week's winner.

I thought, "Oh well, I can pick them up on the drive" and then that 12-year-old's face flashed in front of my eyes. Was I going to be another adult who let these kids down? Another adult who betrayed their trust?

Another person who crapped all over them?

I could not take the chance that I may forget or run late. I had to make sure he got what he earned.

I got out of bed, dressed and drove to the local supermarket and bought a pack of baseball cards.

Your word must be your bond or you run the risk of losing the respect of those in your charge. If that happens, you have nothing. When you say you are going to do something, you do it.

Perhaps it was ingrained in me by my parents or my five years in the ARMY. Wherever it came from, I am glad it showed up.

I could go on and on about how much I loved teaching and how much I learned at the New York State Juvenile Justice Residential Facility; there is enough to fill a book on its own. Some of it's very funny, other stuff would rip your heart out.

One moment I will never forget was watching a solidly built, ripped, 16-year-old weight lifter cradle a clay statue he painted as part of an activity.

It was during the 1992 Olympics, our theme was "Champions," and we purchased clay statues for each student: kiln-fired clay weight lifters, sprinters, basketball players, etc. Each student picked the one they wanted and then painted it.

The students worked a half an hour a day on this project over a two week period. When the paint was dried and the statues were coated with a sealer, each student had a statue that they had carefully painted to take back to their rooms (cells). Some of the projects were truly pieces of art with incredible detail.

We had to convince this 16-year-old that this figurine was his to keep; no one was going to take it. It was his. While most students gently carried it in their hands, he took off his t-shirt and gently wrapped the statue in the shirt and cradled it as if it were a baby.

I wondered what had happened to him in his life that he would believe that he was not worthy of a clay figurine. I cried on my drive home.

In my time there, I also saw courageous acts performed in defense of these young people.

The facility director put his career on the line and risked arrest for refusing to allow one of the young men to return to his home. I remember watching as the New York State Ombudsman and two Monroe County Sheriff's deputies arrived and went into the director's office. I was not privy to the conversation, but it was passed onto the teachers from a very reliable source. It went something like this: One of the residents' sentences expired and the facility director was refusing to let him leave. The ombudsman was there on behalf of the young man's father to collect the young man. The sheriffs were there to arrest the director if he refused to follow orders.

While we could not hear the conversation, it was loud and heated.

The facility director was holding the resident because the resident's father was using the young man as a male prostitute and the director knew it. A 14-year-old boy. The director pleaded for the boy to remain in custody at Oatka Residential Facility to save his life. How could they let this happen? This was not justice. He said this was "injustice."

The ombudsman said no, and the resident had to go, and he did. The group collected the boy and his belongings and left the facility.

It was about 10 AM when they left Oatka and by 6 PM, the length of time to drive from upstate New York to NYC with stops and processing out of the juvenile system, that young man would be on the street as a prostitute. The ironic thing was that the prison was most likely the most stable home life that young man ever experienced. At Oatka he had adults who only wanted him to succeed and grow. Back in the city, he was being used.

I did not see the facility director for the remainder of the day. I admired his courage and his valiant effort to save a life. I still do.

It just struck me that our theme for that summer was "champions."

For that moment and perhaps for the first time in his life, that young man had a champion.

We all knew how that young man's story would end.

Why I (still) teach...

Jamal was one the funniest and smartest students I ever taught. Gregarious, handsome, quick witted, kind, a schmoozer. A father's worst nightmare.

Jamal baffled me, he was from an upper middle-class family, his mother well known in her community and very well respected. He was serving time for breaking and entering, theft, and a series of other things. Fortunately, all were non-violent.

He and I often spoke about life and his choices that put him in prison. I encouraged him to not let this define him.

He would be a fantastic Flat-tire Friend. He was that good.

After finishing my teaching at Oatka Residential Facility in the summer of 1990, I began my public school teaching in Horseheads, NY in the fall of 1990.

I went home on a Friday after finishing two weeks at Horseheads Middle School, and thought to myself, "This is not worth it. What am I doing? Hell, I don't care about the Civil War! How in the world can I get a 13-year-old to care about it?." I was doubting my teaching, I was doubting myself.

I was ready to quit.

I sat on my front porch and thought about how I would tell my principal I was quitting, that teaching was not for me.

"Do I call now or do I wait for Monday?"

I really had no idea. The only thing I did know was that I did not want to be a teacher anymore.

At some point during the thinking process, I opened my mailbox and on top of all the mail was a letter from Jamal.

I saw his name and his return address and my first thought was, "How did a convicted juvenile felon get my address?" I opened the letter and began reading. When the summer session at Oatka Residential Facility had ended, I began teaching at Horseheads and Jamal was released on parole.

In his letter, he thanked me and Bob Shaffer for teaching him that education was not about dates and facts and formulas, but about people and encouraging and pushing them to be better.

Good teachers use their subject material to make better people and he was going to be a better person. He was in school and was planning on pursuing engineering as a career. He was working part-time at an engineering firm in the city.

The letter was a "Thank you" for believing in him and helping him to see his potential.

Jamal's letter forced me to reevaluate not only why I taught, but how I taught. I did not quit. Instead, I went to school on Monday and threw away all the traditional teaching materials other teachers had given me. Jamal reminded me that teaching was about "lighting fires, not filling buckets."

I no longer recognize that guy sitting on the porch on Perine Street in Elmira, New York. For that, I owe Jamal a thank you. I am still teaching and I attribute that to him. He believed in me. He trusted me. He made me want to be better. I am who I am as a teacher largely because of him.

Jamal, if you are reading this, Thank you. Peace my friend.

When it comes to promises, don't make them unless you can keep them. So many people count on us on a daily basis to look out for them, to take care of them, to guide them. To do what we've promised to do. If the people in our charge cannot count on us, then they have nothing.

Time to reflect:
Make it your mission to follow through on every promise you make. If there is the smallest hint you may not follow through, do not promise.

Intervene

You may save a life

"...the highest form of knowledge is empathy,
for it requires us to suspend our egos and live in another's world.
It requires profound purpose larger than the self. " ~Plato

The school I teach in is brand new. It's beautiful, wide hallways, stairwells and open spaces that allow you to look from the 2nd floor to the ground floor.

A few years ago, I was walking down the hall during my lunch and saw two of my students and another student that I did not know standing at the top of the 2nd floor stairs. It was not unusual to see students at that place as the physics teachers often do experiments from the top of the stairs, as it is a wide open space, perhaps 10 feet by 12 feet wide between the staircases. You can see top to bottom, about 35 feet below.

As I approached the three students, I offered my hello and asked what the physics teacher had them doing.

One of the boys quickly wheeled and said, "This is not a physics experiment, Mr. Merritt. I'm so glad you are here."

His eyes, demeanor, tone and his physical position in relation to the girl told me immediately something was amiss.

The other young man who was standing in front of the girl blocking her access to the railing said, "Mr. Merritt, this is Suzy." He only looked at me from the corner of his eye, never fully taking his eyes off the young woman. I looked at her and immediately knew she was in distress. Her glassy eyes and tear stained cheeks told me this was serious.

I could tell by the way the boys were surrounding her that this young lady was going to attempt suicide, one boy was in front of her and one immediately to her side. They knew she was contemplating jumping over the railing from the 2nd floor to the ground floor.

With a quick wave of my hand I ushered the young men a few steps back and stepped towards her, placing myself between her and the railing while the boys stood only a step behind her.

I knew I could not leave the situation and I needed the boys to stay where they were.

It's odd that in that moment, only through eye movement and quick non-threatening hand gestures, the three of us could read each other.

I continued to talk quietly with the young lady and knew she was in a bad place; her speech was slurred and her mannerisms indicated someone contemplating jumping. She continued to take tiny steps toward the railing, looking over. Each time I moved to block her advance and the boys gently stepped toward her. We were not letting this happen.

It seemed like an hour, but it was only a minute or two before another teacher approached. I asked her if she could do me a favor and go to the counseling office and ask a counselor to come up here. I was shocked when she said that she was too busy. She did not read the gravity of the situation and continued on without looking at me.

A few seconds later, which seemed like another hour, I saw another teacher approach and fortunately, I saw it was my wife. She stopped and I said I needed her to stay here, she got it. Enough said. She gently replaced me in my position, and I immediately ran to the counseling office. The boys stayed in their positions.

There was a counselor available and immediately came to the scene. She spoke with this young lady and got her to walk with her away from the stairs to the counseling office.

This story may have ended very badly if those two young men had not acted. The boys intervened. They saved her life.

Once the situation was resolved and we could process, I asked the boys how they knew to act? The boys watched the young woman from a small lounge area about 50 feet away from her and the stairs. The boys said they noticed that she repeatedly approached the railing, stepped up on the base, and looked over to the ground floor, 35 feet below. They told me she did this three or four times, each time stepping higher up and leaning farther and farther over. It was at that time they intervened. They both said it was unspoken, they got up and moved to block her access to the railing. They did not wait. They did not look away. They acted. They saved a life.

The young lady got the help she needed.

There will be a time in your life when you will have to choose to intervene or look away. You don't know when it will happen, but it will happen. There will be a time when your humanity is tested. You cannot fail.

I failed once and vowed to never fail again: I was in a store and could hear the sounds of a young child being hit in the next aisle, I could hear the whack, whack on the child and the cries for the mom to stop. I froze. I did nothing. I failed at humanity.

From that assault, I vowed to never let it happen again, I would intervene.

A few years later, my wife and I were walking into a restaurant. As I got out of the car, I could hear a woman screaming at her young child in the car next to ours. This was not just the ordinary "I am angry at my child" situation. As parents we all have been angry and loud. Instead this was a mom out of control, swearing, and acting in a way that through my teaching experience, I knew was abusive. The child was in danger.

I stepped toward the car and the woman turned on me. She rolled her window down and let the verbal assault fly. I asked if she was OK, did she need some help? The verbal assault intensified. I responded with, "My wife has your license plate number and you will be hearing from Children and Youth Service." She started her car and left immediately.

We contacted the state police and Children and Youth Services immediately and passed on what we saw. All we can hope is that they took the appropriate action.

As teachers we are trained to act and are mandatory reporters. We don't have a choice. But in life, you really don't have a choice either. You must act. You must intervene.

You never know when these situations will happen. But they will happen. These situations are intense, they are disconcerting, they make you cringe. Your adrenaline will course through you, but you have no choice: Intervene.

Update:
The young lady from the first incident was in gym class a few months later and approached one of the boys who was at the railing that day. She said to him, "I think your friend did something very kind for me. Will you tell them thank you and that I am much better now?"

This easily could have ended very differently had two 17-year-olds not intervened.

If two 17-year-olds can step up and intervene, we all can.

No homework.

Know your Zen
Find your Zen

Most of this book focuses on how we can be better people, recognize areas for self improvement and make hard decisions. The world and our lives may be absolutely overwhelming. The world and our lives may be busy with both work and home life. Work life and home life can feel like two full-time jobs.

It is easy to find ourselves feeling stress and struggling for a way to slow down or decompress. To this I say, find your Zen.

Zen is the idea that we are at a point of calm attentiveness, a state of relaxation and ability to let go of many of the things that have troubled us throughout our day.

Most of us call it unwinding or slowing down. Some search for their Zen through alcohol or drugs. That is NOT zen. Substance abuse is no substitute for looking inside to find the natural calmness that inhabits each of us.

Buddhists use meditation in all its forms. I struggle with my focus in meditation. Many who attempt meditation claim it is too difficult; they struggle to clear their mind to find that space of no thought. Many worry they are, "doing it wrong."

There's an old Buddhist joke that goes something like this, "if you are trying to meditate, you are doing it wrong."

In any case, I struggle with meditation.

I love baseball.

My Zen is a baseball field, any baseball field. In person.

Televised baseball may be entertaining but it is not the real deal.

Recently, I was invited to a Division I baseball game at our local university. One of my former students, Tyson Cooper, is on the team and a fantastic player, but more importantly, he is a fantastic person. His younger brother, Jake Cooper, is just as quality and also headed to Division I baseball. (Thanks, Ty and Jake, for the invitation to the game and a great day at the park.)

It is a beautiful field. The baseball park was used until this year as part of the NY-Penn League. The players in the NY-Penn League consisted mainly of college draftees in their first professional experience. The field is surrounded by mountains and the view is magnificent, especially at night.

It is not just this field that I love and find peaceful; it really is all ballfields.

There is something about the perfection of a baseball field: the perfectly manicured grass, the 90-foot base paths, the 60-feet 6-inch pitchers mound, the white lines which define the field of play and the wall in the outfield. It is just perfect.

When I arrived at the baseball park, I was immediately at ease. My worries of the upcoming AP exams for my students vanished. My worries about our daughter's pending job disappeared. I could smell the fresh cut grass and the ballpark food. I could hear the announcer and the pre-game music blasting from the speakers.

I found my seat close to the dugout and spotted my former student on the field.

The game evaporated as I sat with the player's family and talked baseball for nearly three hours. It was nirvana. The family and baseball talk was an added bonus for the night.

I know not everyone has the luxury of 3 hours at a ballpark to clear their head. It does not have to be that long; it can be any amount of time that is just for you. Even 5 minutes can be enough time to clear your head and find a bit of calmness.

I attend many baseball games alone. My wife is not a fan and my daughters have outgrown their desire to spend time with me at the ballpark. It is all OK.

I am at the ballpark.

Eckhart Tolle defines stress as "being here and wanting to be somewhere else." Or, in our intensely connected lives, it is wanting to be left alone but worrying that we need to continually check to see who is texting us, or in some instances, who is not texting us. While I was at the game, I had my phone with me. I never looked at it. I forgot I even had it.

We all need that special place. A place to be at peace, to let go of all things on our mind, a place that we are able to reflect on our lives without the continual need to be somewhere else.

For my wife it is her garden. She plans it all winter and in the spring, she makes it come alive. For some it is a church, mosque, synagogue or temple; for others it is the park and just sitting and taking in all the activity. For some it is a trout stream and fly rod. For others it is a bird watching excursion, a hike, bike ride, row or run.

Wherever or whatever it is, we all need a Zen place. Your Zen place. A place just for you to find your calm.

In this book I have pushed you to look out for others, to consider how our actions impact others, to be kind. Now it is time to look out for you.

Our Zen is self-care.

Our Zen place is our chance to be kind to ourselves. Our ability to help others and be our best selves, begins with taking care of ourselves first. It's not selfish to take time for you. It's self-defense. Taking time to rest and recharge our batteries provides the energy we require to continue our quest to add value everyday.

When our daughter was 4-years-old, she loved Batman. She had a Batman suit and wore it everyday. It was great. What was even better, was that at her age, she recognized that even crime fighters needed a break, some down time, maybe even a nap.

95

When she was tired she would say, "My batteries need to be charged." She would head off and take a nap. An hour or so later, her batteries at full strength and her head clear, she was ready to save Gotham, or at least our house and neighborhood from any nefarious activity. She was pretty good. When our second daughter could walk she became Robin. As long as Robin had her sippy cup, life was good. We have pictures.

So take a cue from a 4-year-old Batman and 2-year-old Robin: when you need a break, take a break, rest, recharge and get ready to do the Superhero run.

Do only what you can do
Superheroes need rest too

Be the light for those in the dark
More wag less bark

But take time just for you
Sitting quietly is what I do

No noise to distract
Only stillness and quiet is my act

Have a beauty day

Love you both give em hell

Time to reflect: Right now, get up and take some time for yourself. Right now. If you can get to your Zen place, do so. At a minimum, do some deep breathing and clear your mind. Self-care is self-defense.

Don't let your tongue make you deaf...
~Native American Proverb

The old adage states that we have two ears and one mouth and that we should speak and listen with respect to this proportionality. We all talk too much, but this isn't only about talking too much, it's about the way we allow our talking and thoughts to crowd out the other person, to make us deaf to their words or needs.

When we are speaking, there is often a linear progression to what we want to say, what we want the other person to know. Most conversations are not conversations, but a series of statements, perhaps by both parties, trying to make or prove a point. Kind of like playing ping-pong against an opponent on different tables.

Sometimes our need to be right and heard results in us attempting to dominate another person; hence, our tongue makes us deaf. We spend our time thinking about what the other person said wrong, or should have said, all the while preparing our response so that we don't take the time to hear what they're actually saying.

I am guilty of this. My wife is very smart and I sometimes hear her speaking but don't hear her words or what she is actually saying. I am rehearsing my response, I am talking in my head. I am aware of this process and am doing what I can to rectify it.

One of the things I have found that helps is what Thich Nhat Hahn calls "deep listening;" it's truly a mindful and active listening technique. Simply, you do your best to focus on your breath, clearing your mind of any possible thing that may interfere with the conversations you are about to have. The other person is your focus and what they have to say is important. Do your best to turn off the soundtrack running through your brain, attempting to anticipate what they are going to say. Instead, intentionally listen to what they are saying. Hear the actual words and their actual meaning, not what you wanted those words to be or what you thought those words meant. The voice in your head is still a voice. Look at the person and make eye contact (not in a creepy way, but in a loving and understanding way). For all you cat lovers, think "soft eyes."

Repeat back to them some of the important things they are saying to make sure your inner voice is not lying to you. Ask questions when necessary. Genuinely seek to understand what they are saying.

Some of you may be thinking that this is simply Active Listening and you are essentially right, but there's an added twist. Deep listening is not only about hearing what was said, it's also about feeling what was said. Letting your mind and thoughts quiet as you devote yourself fully to the other person and what they are saying. If you are looking for ways to make deeper connections, give this a try.

Another way I have limited my over-speaking is simply to ask at the beginning of a conversation, "Do you want advice or do you want an ear?" This approach has helped me limit my interruptions, to listen with clear intention. Asking this kind of question at the start allows you to know what the person needs from you and you can act accordingly. My daughter, the social worker, taught me this in a bit harsher way but with the same effect. During a particularly tough conversation, she said to me, "Dad, I just need you to listen." I got it.

As a dad, and quite probably as a male, we want to fix things. We want to offer advice whether it was solicited or not. I believed, "I am the dad and dad knows best, so listen to me." I am wrong.

I have to continually check myself with my younger daughter. I find myself telling her "how" to handle a situation instead of really hearing what she needs. My wife has helped me with this and I have room for improvement. If it's an ear they want, offer the ear, shut up, and practice deep listening, because they may need the compassion you show in doing so.

If it's advice, again practice deep listening. Wait for the person to finish before offering the advice. Take time to clarify exactly what they are asking for and then go ahead. Advise away.

Time to reflect:
In the next conversation you have, practice deep listening. As best you can, clear your mind, don't anticipate what the other person might say. Look at them and hear what they are saying. Feel what they are saying. My guess is that this practice will allow you to gain deeper understanding and stronger connections with whomever you are hearing.

...or your privilege make you blind

My recognition of my privileges started young. I did not recognize it as privilege, but I knew I was treated differently.

I was in second grade and another boy in the class was having a birthday party. In second grade, all boys are invited to other boys' parties and all girls are invited to all the girls' parties, or at least that is what I thought.

Danny handed me the invitation and said he hoped I could come. I was excited. I headed over to my best friend at the time, Mike. Mike was African American. I asked Mike if he wanted my mom to pick him up or did he want his mom to pick me up and most likely blathered on about what the gift would be, etc.

Mike looked at me and said he did not get one, he was not invited. I was confused. It was a birthday party and all boys were invited to other boys' parties.... I headed over to Danny and said, "Hey did you forget Mike? Where is his invitation?"

Keep in mind, this happened nearly 50 years ago. I cannot remember what I ate for lunch yesterday, but I will never forget this event and the words that Danny said from 50 years ago. He simply looked at me and said, "My dad don't want any N-word at my house."

I can't recall how I responded because those words hit me like a sledgehammer. What did he mean? It was Mike! Why would he say that word? I knew that word and I knew it was not a good word. I didn't understand.

I went home and told my mom what happened, she helped me make sense of it and then she made me make a decision. I remember this part as clearly as I remember what Danny said. My mom asked me, "Andrew, what are you going to do?" (For the record, when she used "Andrew," it was serious.)

My mom, the person who was responsible for teaching me right from wrong, with that question, taught me a life lesson: Always do what is right. Always.

Even at 8-years-old, I knew what was right. Mike came to my house that Saturday, and we had a great time.

As I reflect on this incident, what strikes me is how I recall where I was, who was standing beside me. The noise and the smell. The same is true for my conversation with my mom. We were in the back part of my house off the living room.

The other thing that struck me was how easily that word rolled off Danny's tongue, like it was a word that must have been used frequently and with ease in his world. I am glad I did not live in that world.

I am a white guy. And as Lady Gaga says, "Baby, I was born this way." No apologies. In reality there is nothing I can do about it. It's me. I cannot change it.

Because of my gender and skin color, I have been afforded opportunities other people are denied. That is a fact.

- In the handful of times I have been pulled over for speeding or other traffic infractions, I have never, ever, not once feared for my life.
- I never thought my life could end over rolling through a stop sign.
- I have never feared for my wife's life, when she was stopped, nor my for my daughters'.
- I have never, as far as I know, been followed in a store while shopping.
- Never have I been steered toward or away from any potential future housing decisions.
- Neither I, my wife, or my realtor have been handcuffed while looking at a house that is for sale.

- I have never worried that my résumé may mysteriously disappear from the stack of potential interviews.
- I was never shot for carrying a pellet gun from the sporting goods section of a store to the checkout to purchase it.
- I never had a police officer kneel on my neck, like I was a trophy.
- My ability to love who I love and marry who I want was never at the whim of the state legislature. Or in the case of Kentucky, a county clerk.
- I have never been discriminated against because of my gender identity.
- I never had the "Talk" like my niece has had to have with her beautiful 8-year-old son and will eventually have to have with her new baby. I can't even imagine what that talk is like for a mother who must warn her children about being "too loud" or "too big." To ensure they understand not to appear disrespectful in any way. To teach them to only say "Yes sir and no sir." To insist that they always keep their hands visible and be extra careful when wearing a hoodie.

The list of things that have not happened to me and the things I have not had to do or worry about because I am a man and white and cishet is lengthy, likely unimaginably long, and most likely unlimited.
The best way to measure your privilege, no matter who you are, is in the things you don't have to do or worry about.

I don't apologize for my advantages, but I must publicly recognize it and commit to making sure all people are treated equally. I have an obligation to make the world a better place for all.

Today, too many people refuse to recognize their privilege. I suggest you don't need to apologize for your privilege; simply recognizing it is the first step to creating a more equitable and just society.

There is an old saying, attributed to many different people: "Too many people were born on third base and think they hit a triple." Perhaps it's the baseball metaphor, but this simple saying has stuck with me for years. We must recognize that all of us are at different starting points. Not everyone has two parents in a stable home, not everyone has food and a bed, not everyone has clean clothing, some fear going home because it is an unsafe environment.

About ten years ago, I had a young lady in my class who was very thoughtful and genuinely kind. I really like her and still stay in contact occasionally. This was an AP US Government class and we were discussing the 1964 Civil Rights Act and if it should be updated to fit 2010 US. This young lady raised her hand and said, "The way to end discrimination is to travel, to go to other countries and interact with peoples of all cultures and races."

She then went on about her recent trip to the Dominican Republic and her next trip to Switzerland.

I knew what she meant and her sentiment had merit, but what she failed to realize was that she was starting on third base. Her father was the CFO of a major corporation.

I looked quickly around the room and saw the looks of confusion on several faces and before any student could drop a bomb on her, I gently said, "I understand your argument but not everyone starts at the same place, not everyone can travel like you are able."

Her look spoke volumes.

She genuinely did not recognize her starting point. She was not being malicious, she just did not get it. Because of who her father was, she had far greater opportunities and advantages than most every other student. She had not earned her position, she was born into it. She was born on third base and did not recognize it.

Lastly, this year, I was having a conversation with some students about my high school years and how I had a pretty good life. I mentioned I had two parents, a decent school, no trouble with the law, never had to rob a store to feed my sister, I had solid academic opportunities, always had ample job opportunities and a bit of money from that work, always had food and a place to live, did not have to pay my car insurance, in fact had a car that my parents provided for me, etc. Without missing a beat, one of those students, Natalie, looked at me, smiled, and reminded me of my advantages and my life's starting point with a simple, "Hey Merritt, you do know you are a white male?"

I laughed and told Natalie she was right.

It really is that easy. Again no need to apologize, just begin with recognition.

Time to reflect:
Read Ta-Nehisi Coates, "Between the World and Me" and when you are ready, and you want your mind blown, pick up anything by James Baldwin. By far the most brilliant writer I have ever read. His words cut you and you don't know you are bleeding.

We all can't be in the parade
Know your role

I don't even like parades, never did.

It's nice to be the star, the one everyone wants to see, the star of the show.

We all can't be stars.

Ask the stars. They will be the first to say that it's the behind-the-scenes people that make them who they are. It's the gaffer and the grip. (OK, I don't know what those things are but they are on every credit roll.)

Ask the news anchor or correspondent and they will immediately point to the producer. Ask the pitcher and they point to the pitching coach; the .330 hitter and it's the hitting coach. (For the baseball references, see how long you last in the show by claiming you did it on your own.)

The list of those supporting the stars is endless. No support people, no stars, and no parade.

There is no shame in any job…

Only the shame you bring to it.

In my life I worked several jobs and, in all honesty, I loved them all. My first job, besides working on my parents' small vegetable farm, was doing field maintenance at a softball complex. My main role was preparing the fields for the games and then relining and preparing the fields for the next games. There were three fields and each field was used for four games a night. It was a busy job as the games would often end at about the same time so I had to hustle to each field to get it ready.

In the late 1970s and into the early 1980s, slow-pitch softball was very popular. While it was not the most glamorous job, I was outside all day most weekdays, and all day on weekends for the softball tournaments.

I got to know many people and got to play a lot of softball. But most of all, I grew up and took on a lot of responsibility. By the time I was 17, I was there full-time during the summer and had two people who worked for me. I worked there until I left for the ARMY in 1983.

During the summer of 1983, prior to leaving for basic training, I worked both at the softball complex full-time and for our village roads department, also full-time. 80 hours a week.

I was busy.

At the village department, I did all types of odd jobs, mowing and whatever the boss instructed. Friday was always garbage day—that was fun. I and a good friend rode on the garbage truck and collected all the garbage in our village. We started at 6 AM, normally finished by 1PM, and were done for the day.

You can learn a lot about people from their garbage. You know who may have an alcohol problem or who eats a lot of fast food. You get an up-close look at what types of magazines people read. Remember, this is pre-Internet.

While many may look down on sanitation workers, the job is vital. Watch what happens when a sanitation crew goes on strike in a city. I am impressed with the sanitation workers in my community. They are professional in every sense. In fact, on the rare occasion when I forget to get ours to the curb, they will come and take the cans from the corner of the garage.

After that 80-hour-a-week summer, it was off to the ARMY.

Well, the ARMY is the ARMY. Basic training was the toughest intentional mental and physical challenge I faced. And before I left, my dad offered me two pieces of advice:
- Don't volunteer for anything
- Don't let them learn your name.

I did my best to heed his advice.

I almost made it through the name thing until the last day of basic training when one of the drill sergeants called me out during our return march from the PX to buy clothing and supplies as we prepared to graduate and move on to Advanced Individual Training (AIT).

The drill sergeant called me out and said to me, "I bet you thought I did not know your name." I replied, "That's true, drill sergeant." Within 15 seconds of leaving the PX, I had the platoon completely out of step. He called me out and just as quickly sent me back into the formation. Calling cadence was not my strength.

My take away from the ARMY was that you can accomplish many things you never thought possible: Rappelling, weapons training, live fire exercises, 1, 2, and 3 rope bridges, CS gas chamber, just to name a few. At the same time, you make some of the strongest connections of your life and build lifelong relationships. I am still in contact with a number of people with whom I served. The bonds you build are unbreakable.

My ARMY experience instilled in me a few valuable life lessons:
- Every person and every job is critical to mission success. The mechanic who doesn't do preventive maintenance on an armored vehicle endangers every person in it. Every soldier, marine, coastie, seaman, or airman depends on every other person. We all want the best parachute riggers rigging our parachutes. Yes, that is a job.
- Every person has value. While I may not have been the best marksman, I could use maps well and get us to the rally point, if necessary. Oh yeah, cooks. Cooks are really important. In all honesty, the best food I ever ate was in the ARMY.
- The ARMY is far more egalitarian and open than most think. For anyone needed anything, it never mattered if the person providing for that need or working on the equipment was Muslim, gay, or trans, etc.
- In the ARMY, you don't care what somebody is, you care if they can do their job well. That is it.
- Although I was never in any type of real combat situation, I cannot think a wounded marine laying in a street in Afghanistan will ask the corpsman tending her wounds if he is gay. The only thing that matters is whether that person can save that life.

- I also developed a "Finish the job" attitude, and cultivated the characteristic of being the "closer." When you begin a job, finish the job, do the job well, and be proud of the job you did. It's that simple.
- We are all in this life together. Every person has strengths and weaknesses. Capitalize on the strengths and work to improve known weaknesses.
- Leave no person behind. I remember finishing a 2-mile run with a buddy and heading over to the drill sergeant to show off our time. He never looked at us, he only said, "There are still soldiers out on that track." We got it. Back out we went to encourage those still running.
- The film, Black Hawk Down, best illustrates this military way of life. Soldiers refuse to leave the fight until the pilots of the downed helicopter are recovered.
- Leaving people behind is one area where our society fails and the military excels. Imagine how much better this world would be if we "left no one behind."

Gandhi said that the true measure of any society can be found in how it treats its most vulnerable members.

In my current job as a teacher, some of the best advice I received early on was, "Don't piss off the custodians or secretaries/assistants." Those roles are the guts of any school.

I know of one retired administrator who made hiring decisions based on how well they treated the assistant in the office prior to the interview. The administrator asked the assistant their thoughts on the candidates.

Tim Mnichin is a New Zealand comedian and he talks about how he makes decisions about his career by how the producers and agents treat the wait staff in the restaurant as they are discussing business. I love his line: "I don't care if you are the most powerful cat in the room; I will judge you on how you treat the least powerful. So there."

Our jobs and career choices can define us or we can define them.

Time to reflect:
Think of all the jobs you have had. Identify your takeaways; identify how the job informed who you are today.

Take care of the people who take care of your people

Everyone wants to be recognized for their work. A paycheck is nice but it is the intangibles, the cards, the handwritten notes —those little extras — that truly make you feel valued.

Throughout my teaching career, I've kept all the many gifts and notes I received, my favorites being the handwritten notes that detail an event or an interaction I had likely forgotten but stuck with the student.

Saying thank you can be as simple as when my dad was in the hospital for an extended time. Each time we visited we would take the staff some sort of thank you treat. It may have been donuts or a cake, not anything extravagant, but a gesture to say thank you to let everyone know how grateful we were for the continued care of our dad.

My mom entered an assisted living community in 2018. Although she worried it was her memory that prompted this move, the transition was really about providing the necessary care for her physical ailments that we, her family, lacked the ability and expertise to provide. I've learned that, as parents age, it's important to recognize our limitations and get them the help we cannot provide. Stealing a line from Phyllis Vance from the Office: "And if you wait for the day when a parent comes to you and says 'I can't take care of myself anymore' it's never gonna happen."

In 2018, my mom spent six nights in the hospital just before Christmas. I was the only child available to be with her. I packed my bag and off to Rochester I went. Each day I visited I took a treat for the staff working that day. It was such a simple thing and the staff was very thankful. Every day.

I quickly realized how important the staff and caregivers were at her assisted living community. They were invested in her care and wellbeing. When my mom entered the hospital and I would need to stop by her apartment to pick something up, every staff member would ask about "Annie" and when she would be coming home.

I realized this was her new home and they were her new family. I was OK with that. I was thankful for them.

We need to make sure we respect, acknowledge and thank those doing the hard jobs.

My mom's last few years were richer and better because she had the round-the-clock care she needed. As much as I wanted to believe that she would have been better off with a family member, I know that was not true.

LPN's, nursing assistants, and aides— their work is heroic. This group is the backbone of an assisted living or skilled nursing facility. When you need to know what is really going on, talk to them.

My sister was on a first name basis with the entire staff. While sometimes family members may become a hindrance as staff does their job, not my sister. The staff knew she knew my mom better than anyone. They valued and respected her input.

They also knew she respected them and that she was thankful for their care and compassion in very difficult situations.

As COVID began to spread, I made several bracelets and necklaces and sent them to my mom to give to "her people," the ones who showed up every day to care for her.

She did not receive the package until after her COVID diagnosis. Unfortunately, COVID took hold of her before she could hand them out.

My sister was speaking with the staff during this time and they told her a package arrived for my mom and they did not know what to do with it. My sister told them to open it and share the different items as this is what my mom wanted. They were very appreciative of the small tokens of thanks.

Our goal was simply to thank those who take care of our family members. After my mom died, I called the owner of the facility and told him about the care my mom received and listed the professionals by name that took care of her in her final hours.

I told the facility owner that my mom's favorite aide was with her when she died. He served as a surrogate brother for me. I never personally met this man but I am forever indebted to him. My sister said he was a young man, full of life, who took the time to get to know his patients. He asked my mom about her life and my dad's life and was especially interested in the collage of pictures of my dad that my wife made for his funeral.

The aide listened to the stories my mother shared about my father and said he was an amazing man. He was shocked to learn my dad was a .50 caliber machine gunner in the Korean war and survived.

He made my mom's final hours peaceful and he stayed with her until the end.

Time to reflect: Make a list of the people who take care of your people and call them, write to them, or send a small gift to let them know you value them, appreciate them, and just want to say THANK YOU.

Little victories

Learn to measure and celebrate life in little victories.

A baby can't walk until they stand, they can't stand until they crawl.

These are the little victories. Every parent knows this.

As a teacher, this is my world.

When students arrive in my classroom, they are my kids and I will do whatever it takes to get them through the class and to graduation. I teach mainly senior level classes. Most of these students are in "coast" mode and just looking to June and graduation. A good number of them show up with a "tell me what needs to be done so I can graduate" type of attitude.

Every now and then you find a student who, for whatever reason, is willing to forsake the previous 12 years of education and quit.

Prior to my first year of teaching in the high school, I had spent the previous 12 years at the middle school level. My first year at the high school I taught a course called Problems of Democracy (POD). One of my students was a young man who did not value education—at least not the formal kind.

His interest was cars and he wanted to work designing and engineering them. He was very good. One day I noticed he was not in class for three days in a row. I asked the class if anyone knew if he was OK. Was he sick? A student answered, "He quit."

"Quit what?" I asked.

"School" was the answer.

"Not happening" was my immediate thought; he had four months left to graduate.

I called the counseling office to verify that he quit. He, in fact, had quit.

I called him. It was about 9:15 AM and whomever answered the phone said that he was sleeping.

I asked them to wake him up. I was his teacher and I was checking on him.

I could hear the person on the phone yell at him to wake up. I could hear him ask who it was and what did they want?

They said, "It's your teacher."

I heard, "Aww shit!"

He got on the phone and asked what I wanted. It was simple, I told him. "Quitting is not an option and I expect you to be in school."

He responded, "I quit and am not coming back."

I then told him I would call him everyday until he came back to school. I don't think he believed me. So began a two-week episode of me calling him every morning, sometimes before school, sometimes after the first period class. Every conversation was similar to the one above.

Then it happened. He walked into class one morning. All I said was, "Welcome back."

He graduated. A little victory.

I had a similar situation with a student I knew from middle school so I already had a connection. Now he was in my AP US Government class. This kid was the real deal. He had all the academic skills. He simply quit coming to school. And so while he did not formally quit, he just stopped showing up.

After the third day of not showing up to my class, I asked if anyone knew anything about him? Was he sick? A couple of students shot each other a quick look, and finally one student said, "He is just not showing up. I don't know why."

I called and spoke with his counselor. He said the mom does not know how to get him to school; she tries everything and he will not get out of bed. I asked the counselor if he wanted to go for a ride. Off we went. Before we left, we called the mom and told her we were on our way to get him out of bed. She agreed. We arrived, knocked, went to his room and told him that it was time for school. "Get up and get dressed."

I was unsure what would happen, but to my surprise he did. We stopped and grabbed him some breakfast at a convenience store on the way back to school.

In retrospect, he may have been struggling with a mental health issue. I knew him and this was very unusual behavior. The counselor and I repeated the drive to his house maybe five more times. I was prepared to do this all semester if need be. No one quits school, at least without a fight from me.

It worked. He started attending regularly. A little victory. From that day on, anytime he missed school, he got a call. On the rare occasion he missed, his mom assured me he was genuinely sick.

Update: This young man graduated from high school, graduated from college and went on to a masters. He needed to know he had value. He was supported and we genuinely cared about him.

Have I convinced every student who wanted to quit school to stay? No. That does not stop me from trying nor should it stop you.

Our young people are an investment. To allow them to quit school or harm themselves is a loss to us as a society. As Sitting Bull said, we have one responsibility: "to take care of the children."

Many young people are very capable and they just don't realize it. Some are unable to recognize their capabilities maybe because of a past trauma or because they feel "less than."

My job as a teacher is to make them see what they can accomplish. When I see that young person come to life, it's a little victory.

My experiences at the juvenile prison taught me this and for the past 32 years that has been my goal. If students also happen to learn something about the US Government along the way, that is a bonus.

You can't always win the war but you can definitely take solace in the little victories you help make happen along the way.

Little victories take many forms. In life we often think we need to be already great at something in order to do that thing. That is not true. Even the best athlete would struggle to run a marathon without training. So measure the buildup to the marathon, and count each training session as a victory as you build towards the marathon.

If you're not a runner, start with a walk. Little victory. The next day, walk a bit further. Little victory. Build in a few hundred yards of slow running. Little victory. Add in a half mile slow run with the walk. Little victory.

I think you see where this is going.

Use this same approach in every aspect of your life. Want to learn to play guitar? Just know that you are not Jimi Hendrix or Prince. Yet.

But maybe one day.

Start with a chord. Practice it. Little victory. Add in another chord. Practice it. Little victory. Add in a third chord. Practice it. Little victory.

And now you have a song. That is a win.

Apply this to art. Not Picasso. Yet.

Want to learn a new language? YouTube search it. Start small—a few words and phrases. Little victories. And then challenge yourself to real conversation. You will mess up. That is OK. Do it again and again.

I was a Russian linguist in the military. I could tell you if we were being invaded but could not order in a restaurant. I spent the past few years practicing conversational Russian. I suggest, "Russian with Max." You can find it online.

Recently, I walked into the main office of my school and was hit with a Russian, "Shto eto?" In English, this means, "What is this?" The person standing before me was referring to the hockey sweater I was wearing. It was the 1980 Soviet Olympic Hockey Jersey of Vladislav Tretyak with the CCCP embroidered on the chest.

The person who asked is the assistant to the equity director at school and she is Czech. She learned Russian as a child in Czechoslovakia. We broke into a basic discussion of the jersey and also how I knew Russian. I wasn't perfect, not even close. She was very kind, helping me along with the language.

The staff was amazed as we spent five or so minutes speaking only in Russian. My little victory.

Author Malcolm Gladwell argues that it takes 10,000 hours to master any skill.

Time to reflect:
Get to it. Start practicing…. something.

Sign the goddamn paper, Andrew

All of us, every single person reading this will face or has already faced the most agonizing of decisions. Personally, I can think of nothing more excruciating than an end-of-life decision. I hope, for your sake, your decision is made easier by pre-planning and preparation.

September 19th, 2008 was one of the best and worst days of my life. I will never forget it. Ever.

My dad was very sick. Sepsis had set in. He was in the hospital and we all knew this was most likely the end.

Earlier in the morning, before I, my mom and other siblings went to the hospital, we met with my mom's minister from St. Andrew's Epicopal Church. He went through the obligatory ministerial things. A prayer and discussion of god's love, etc. He then discussed how my dad had made his death as easy on all of us as one possibly could. My mom and dad both had living wills and advanced directives that spelled out specifically what was to happen if they were incapacitated and, sadly, he was incapacitated. He had made the decisions for us.

My dad was a diabetic, and a terrible diabetic patient at that. He ate whatever he wanted and used insulin to offset his bad eating habits. He really liked doughnuts, cake, and pie. If you don't know, diabetes is insidious and attacks the blood flow into the extremities—the hands and feet.

About six months earlier, he had a toe amputated because it was gangrenous. I went with him and my mom to the surgeon as they discussed the surgery.

The doctor, a very nice man, said they had to do this. If they did not the gangrene would spread rapidly. The best course of action was to amputate the toe.

My dad looked at my mom and said, "Annie, what do you think?"

She said, "George, we really have no choice."

My dad agreed and looked at the doctor and said, "Doc, you get one body part, make it count." We all laughed, but all knew this was probably only the beginning. And for my dad, well, he meant it.

My dad also suffered from small vessel disease. This neurological issue closed off the vessels of the brain where his short-term memory was stored. He had limited memory of anything dating from his present moment to about 10 years back. The hardest thing was that he knew he lost his memory and was embarrassed by it.

When we visited, we got used to my dad asking repeatedly how long ago it was that we had arrived. He knew all of us but he could not remember the minute before. It bothered him, no one else.

The doctor did the surgery, amputated the toe and my mom helped him rehab. The loss of the toe severely limited his already limited mobility.

My mom was a saint. In addition to caring for my dad, she also cared for my sister who was diagnosed with ovarian cancer and a brother who was in a severe airplane crash. She never once complained about any of it.

Throughout the summer, my sister steadily improved and my dad steadily declined. We all knew where this would end. We gathered at my parents' apartment that September morning, listened to the minister, and then all headed to the hospital. It was going to be, at best, days, not weeks. We arrived— my mom, me, both my older brothers, older sister, and younger sister.

The doctor met with us and told us the infection causing the sepsis was rapidly attacking my dad's leg and that if action were not taken immediately, meaning another amputation, he would die.

The doctor knew of the living will and advanced directives, yet still implored us to consider the amputation. As a family, we discussed it and knew there was really nothing we could do. His legal document superseded anything we wanted.

I was standing with my mom in the hallway outside my dad's room when the surgeon approached once again. He had a surgical suite reserved and could have my dad in surgery in minutes. He could get us at least six more months.

I looked at my mom.

Her look told me everything I needed to know. The answer was "No." She thanked the doctor and said she understood he was doing his job; he was a surgeon, and he wanted to save her husband.

He said he understood and then handed my mom a clipboard and pen. On the clipboard was a legal document indicating that as my dad's wife and proxy, she was refusing any further treatment. My mom took the pen, and then thinking out loud said, "We have had 54 beautiful years together. I spent the night with him last night and he knows how I feel. I will see him again, and he will be waiting." She signed the paper.

I thought, "Damn mom, you are the toughest person I know."

Before I could step away and cry, the doctor said, "We need a witness to your mom's signature."

My mom handed me the pen.

Behind the doctor stood three nurses. Once the legal documents were signed, they would unhook everything from my dad except pain medication. He would die. Meanwhile, my mom was handing me the pen to sign a document that would end his life.

She must have seen the hesitation in my face. I was searching the hallway for my brothers and sisters. Where were they? I did not want to sign this paper.

"Andrew," she said. "Andrew" was as serious as it got.

Then I heard it.

"Sign the goddamned paper, Andrew." It was my dad.

I could hear my dad's words in my brain. He swore a lot. The pain medication and infection made him largely non-communicative, but his lessons were speaking to me.

He was demanding I fulfill the lessons he taught me. He was saying to me "This is not about you, this is about me and I can't do it myself. You must do this. This is not a time to be selfish, this a time to be selfless. Be a Good Man."

His lessons spoke volumes.

I had an obligation to do the right thing. The right thing was to sign the paper. "Sign the goddamn paper", I heard it again in my head. He had done his job, he had brought me to this point and my obligation was to sign the paper. I could not be selfish. "Sign the paper." He was OK, he was tired, and he was ready. "Sign the paper."

I knew by signing that paper he would die. My father and best friend would be gone.

I signed the paper.

The three nurses entered the room and disconnected everything except pain medication and prepared to move him to hospice.

Everyone knew it would be quick as the infection continued to rapidly spread.

So how was this one of the best and worst days?

The worst-day part is pretty obvious. The man I loved more than any other was going to die and I signed the paper.

The best day? Well my dad was sick, very sick. No matter how much my mom tried, his quality of life was slipping—not because she was not doing all she could, but because he was wearing out. He was tired and it was time for him to go.

My readings on Buddhism taught me that George F. Merritt, Jr. is not gone. He is me, he is my sister. In Buddhism, one does not die, they change form. Just as we cannot come from nothing, we cannot become nothing.

I am everything my dad and mom were. I am them.

When we lose someone close—a parent, brother, sister or friend—they are never gone. Everything they are and all they have done is in us.

I encourage anyone reading this to read Atul Gawande's *Being Mortal* and anything by Thich Nhat Hahn to help make sense of death and the decisions families must make. They are powerful.

I was with my dad when he died.

He was moved to hospice. It was a beautiful place. Quiet and serene. There were no blinking lights or beeping sounds, no calls for doctors and nurses to immediately report to a room, no hospital smell. Everyone there knew why they were there and that this place was their final destination. It was peaceful.

My dad was brought in, and I was with my mom as they completed the admittance papers. Even that process was done with the utmost care and respect—quiet voices asking important questions. The only purpose was to make my dad's final days, or hours, as we would find out, as easy as possible. After he was checked in and given a room, our family decided someone should be with him at all times as we all knew his time was limited. Since I traveled the farthest distance and did not yet have a hotel to stay in, I volunteered.

My family said their goodbyes and headed back to their houses as they all lived fairly close by or had a place to stay locally.

I sat in a chair very close to my dad; he was completely non-communicative partly due to the infection, but more so due to the pain medication.

I turned the Yankee-Orioles game on and watched. He loved baseball as much as I do. I was doing my best to give him play-by-play in the event he could hear me. Derek Jeter came to the plate and laced a single between short and second. I looked over at my dad and said, "Look at that dad, Jeter singled."

My father always professed to dislike Derek Jeter, he called him "Jeters." In reality, my dad loved Derek Jeter. Jeter was a gamer. He showed up to the field everyday and gave the game his all. Jeter never used "I" when talking about an accomplishment or World Series win. My dad respected the humble players.

My dad took a sharp, deep, long breath, exhaled, and died. I knew it immediately.

I have heard about out of body experiences but never experienced one, until that second.

I remember being pulled from my body up into the corner of the room watching as my physical body checked for a pulse, there was none. As quickly as I was pulled from my body, I was back.

I went to the desk and told the nurse I believed my dad had died. I did not know how to say it because I never had to say it before. I just said, " I think my dad....died." The nurse quietly said, "Let's check on him."

The nurse entered the room, checked his pulse, pulled his stethoscope from around his neck, listened for a heart beat and gently placed his ear to my dad's nose and mouth and felt for a pulse. He looked at me and said, very kindly and quietly, "He is gone." He noted the time and then lit a candle.

The people who work in hospice care are not superheroes, they are superhuman. They are the warriors that Sitting Bull talks about. They deal with people and families at their absolute worst times and show kindness and compassion beyond anything I can imagine.

They do it with dignity showing respect for those suffering, at their worst. I wonder who takes care of them in their times of crisis? I am thankful for them.

Knowing your "Why" is one thing. Carrying it out is another.

Signing that paper was me living my "Why." For me that was the ultimate "Good man" moment.

As I reflect on that moment, I can still hear the hospital noise and smell the antiseptic. I can feel the pen in my hands as I scribbled my name and date. It was difficult but it was right. It was what Good Men do.

Time to reflect:
All of us will face that "Why" moment. We will be tested and we must answer the call. Hard things are hard because they are hard.

If you know your "Why," doing your duty is easier. Not easy.

Take care of your mother

My dad's last words: "Take care of your mother." He could barely speak, but I heard it. The nurses were preparing to move him so he could be transported to hospice. He even raised his hand and pointed at us.

For almost 12 years after his death, I did all I could to live up to his instruction.

But this is an area where I still carry doubt. I wonder if I really did enough? This may also be an area of my life in which I need to be more kind to myself.

After my dad died, my mom lived alone in the Rochester area. For a number of years, she lived in an apartment, drove, visited with friends and relatives went out to dinner. I really think she enjoyed her life and freedom.

In the spring of 2017, she had a serious fall. She was unable to get up and her Life Alert was in her bedroom. She could not get to it. She sat on the bathroom floor for a number of hours until a neighbor knocked and wondered where she was. She was able to get the neighbor's attention and the neighbor immediately called 911.

That event was the final event in a series of falls that led the family to "have the talk" with her about finding an alternative living situation.

My brother declared that she would live with him, three hours away from her friends and family in Rochester and nearly an additional three hours drive for us to visit in Alexandria Bay, New York.

While I was relieved that she would have a safe place to live, I was worried about the psychological toll of going from nearly complete freedom and independence to a living situation where she would lose a good part of that. She would also lose the friend and familial connections she enjoyed her entire life.

For years, I called my mom at least twice a day. The first time on my drive home from school. Nothing profound. Just a quick run down of our days, small talk, weather stuff, etc.

I would again call at night and talk about the news and any other topics that seemed interesting. She loved sports and although did not follow closely, was a Buffalo Bills fan. I did my best to make her a Yankee fan.

As her year at my brother's progressed, I noticed her spark, her zest, beginning to wane. Perhaps it was her age. She was 83. I think it was more likely that she was so far away from her home, friends, and other grandchildren. She was active in Alexandria Bay— her new home— but not nearly as active as she was in Rochester.

She had a car but it was best she did not drive. Her independence was limited.

This has to be a difficult thing to know.

My brother and his family took great care of her, provided everything she needed and more. They even built a bedroom and private bath out of a dining room.

In the year and half she spent there, we visited four or five times. Never enough, but all we could do.

In the fall of 2018, her needs were more than my brother could provide. I suggested she look into an assisted living home in the Rochester area.

While she could not drive, her friends and relatives could visit her. After some family angst, it was arranged, and she moved back to Rochester.

She moved into a very nice facility. I visited her and helped her organize all her clothing and put it all away as it had been left in suitcases and boxes.

My sister came the following week and really got things in order.

For the next year-and-a-half, the phone calls increased to three times a day: on the way to school, after school and one last evening call to say good night. She even mastered Facetime and found a way to add my sister to our calls. The morning call was a great way to start my day.

With her living in Rochester, we visited far more often and my sister visited three and sometimes four times a week. While we could see her slowly physically deteriorating, her mind was sharp and she could still dish out a good zing. Her main issues were physical; walking and standing were difficult.

While at the assisted living home, she had another fall and this facility wasn't equipped to care for her physical needs.

So again, in the fall of 2019, she moved. This time to a skilled nursing facility. While this facility was not as beautiful as the first, it was very nice. The staff was magnificent.

It was then, though, that she really began to keep to herself. She ate in her room and rarely ventured out. She was also tiring more quickly and her interest in crosswords and solitaire had diminished, although she did develop a serious love of funny cat videos that she would watch for hours on her iPad. She, like my sister and daughter, loved cats.

On one occasion while we were visiting her, she asked me to retrieve something from a drawer by her bed. I opened the drawer and it was filled with candy. She called it her "Loot drawer." I asked her about it and she smiled. All she said was that Jon, my sister's husband, took good care of her. I took a piece and handed her one.

At 85 nearly 86, you are entitled to candy at any time. She, like my dad, had mastered the insulin offset to enjoy the small pleasures in life…. candy.

In the last year-and-a-half years of her life, when she first moved back to the Rochester area, I saw my mom come back. The spark, the zest. She was definitely in physical decline but her mind was sharp and her love of all things political came back. She was a social justice warrior before being a social justice warrior was cool. I believe our oldest daughter inherited this from my mom.

We talked frequently about the state of our nation and I assured her it would get better.

The last time we visited in person was late February of 2020.

Then COVID.

Her facility locked down on March 13. My phone calls increased to sometimes five or six times per day. It must have been difficult to not be allowed to leave your room; I imagine it might have felt a little like prison.

She never complained. She said the staff was doing all they could to keep everyone safe, in good spirits, and well fed.

Then I got the call. Wednesday, April 8 at 3:32PM. I remember the specific time because I was teaching online and my phone rang and I saw my sister's name. I thought, "I will call her back when I am done." I clicked "off."
And then it rang again. I thought it was a mistake; she had to have accidentally called again. I clicked "off."

And then a third time.

This could not be a mistake. I ended my class.

I answered and she told me that mom tested positive for COVID and was refusing treatment. She and my mom had spoken at length and in detail as to what her decision meant. My mom was aware and fully cognizant.

I told my sister I would call my brothers. We ended the call quickly and I then immediately called my mom.

I spoke with her about COVID and what it would most likely do. She was aware and she was not afraid. I am certain she made some biblical reference; she was a woman of strong faith. I do not recall. I was trying my best to hold back my emotions.

I was amazed at how resolute she was. She was at peace. There was no changing her mind. I had to make peace with that.

That was the last time I spoke with her in any coherent way. COVID was unmerciful, and I noticed the next morning when I called how her breathing was more labored and her mind was not as sharp.

I called a former student of mine, now a Flat-tire Friend of mine, a doctor, and he explained the medical team most likely had started some sort of pain medication, and that could be the cause of the confusion and slow recall. He also warned me not to take anything she said literally. This COVID monster was vicious and, mixed with pain medication, anything she said may be nonsense.

My brother called me early Friday morning and told me that mom did not have COVID. He had just spoken with her; he said she sounded good and that she did *not* have COVID. I sent him a screenshot of the test from the University of Rochester hospital showing the COVID diagnosis. She *had* COVID.

My doctor friend's warning was coming true.

I called her and she told me the same thing: No COVID.

I said OK and tried to talk about other things, but the medication was doing a job on her. I was glad just to hear her voice.

My thoughts went to my dad and I wondered what he would tell me to do. I wondered if I had "taken care of my mother." And I heard his voice again. It wasn't "Sign the goddamn paper," it was "Let her go."

I was doubting whether I had done enough to take care of her and wondered if I should go to Rochester and attempt to see her. My wife assured me there was nothing to be done. She was right.

On Monday, April 13, 2020 at 5:35pm, I got the call.

My sister told me mom was gone.

But like my dad, she was not really gone because I am still here, my sister is still here, and her grandchildren are still here. She will never be gone.

In end-of-life moments, we question if we did enough—if we did the right thing in looking out for and caring for those in our charge. There is a lot of self-doubt and, in some cases, guilt. Did I visit enough? Did she know how important she was to me? Did she know that she was the strongest person I have ever known? Did she know that I was in awe of her and that I loved her?

We have to believe we did our best. We have to accept that we took care of those in our charge to the best of our ability. I believe she knew. And that is enough.

There is a powerful scene at the end of the film, Saving Private Ryan. Private Ryan, now grandfather Ryan, is standing looking at the graves of men who died that were charged with bringing him back to his family. You can see the trepidation and doubt in his eyes. Was he enough? Did he earn it? He turns to his wife and asks her if was a good man? Was he worthy of the sacrifice of those other men? Did his life square theirs? And while he knows it is true, yes he squared the debt, sometimes it is nice to hear it. You are enough.

Do not beat yourself up. Do your best. Do not let others make you feel as if you are inadequate or not doing the right thing. Be true to yourself and always take care of your mom.

Trusting that you did your best is enough.

My mom would call me frequently before she died. I kept all my mom's voicemails and I still listen to them. Some of them are funny as she is unaware that she reached my voicemail. Technology was not her thing. But more than anything, just the sound of her voice provides peace.

I owe a huge debt of gratitude to my sister Sally and brother-in-law, Jon. It was my sister's efforts in monitoring my mom and her medications in the last year-and-half that drastically improved and lengthened my mom's life. My sister was vigilant—calling and checking with the nursing staff, asking about drug interactions and other things far beyond my comprehension. Her tenacity in my mom's care gave me peace of mind.

My sister's husband, Jon, was my mom's favorite. He won my mom over quickly by taking incredible care of my sister who was also a diabetic by learning all he could about diabetes from the minute they began dating, and nursing her through three brain surgeries. He also stocked my mom's "Loot" drawer. That alone may have been enough. It was their combined efforts that gave my mom the best quality of life one could ask for.

On another note, if you have older parents, you must have the difficult conversations and ensure you understand their wishes. Consider a Living Will and Advanced Directives, and make sure someone takes on the awesome responsibility of being a healthcare proxy. My sister took this role by default and I could not be more thankful.

Preparing for our own eventual end may be difficult, but it makes the end far easier, especially for those left behind. And honoring your loved ones' final wishes is the ultimate act of love, no matter how painful it might be.

Sometimes love means letting go when all you want to do is hold tighter.

Time to reflect:
Call your parents or another loved one and tell them you love them.

We are only visiting
Act like a guest

When we visit another person, we are normally on our best behavior. We are thoughtful, patient, kind and considerate. We offer to help pick up any dishes or clean up after dinner. That is the right thing to do. For most of us it is natural.

I suggest we apply that same approach more broadly to our lives and all our interactions with others. After all, we're only visiting. Our visit is finite.

In my life I employ the "Do all you can, as often as you can, for as many as you can" approach. I know my time here is limited and that things I put off may never get accomplished.

I am talking about the little things. Every chance you get to say something nice, say it.

- Be effusive in your praise.
- Never underestimate the power of a compliment.
- Look for ways to help.
- My mom taught me this. She said the best compliment she received as a parent is when an acquaintance remarked that all her children were the first to ask if he needed any help. It matters.
- In reality it is not the actual help that matters. What matters is that you asked.

I volunteer every week at our school's food distribution. I have directed traffic, loaded vehicles, pushed carts full of food and milk, whatever the director needs. I know my role. I started volunteering two days after my mom's death. Volunteering helped me. I had to do something.

More importantly, though, is that in the case of feeding a nation in the midst of a crisis, there are no small jobs. Every job is critical if we're to hand out 13,000 meals in a two-hour time window. If the person delivering the milk is slowed, the process stops. If the person directing traffic makes a mistake, someone could get hurt.

The food service director is an amazing woman. She could have planned the Berlin Airlift. She is humble, always redirecting the praise she receives to her team. She understands and lives the belief that she did not build it; it takes a team. Know your role.

When I was a kid, I hated that my mom talked to everyone. And I mean she talked to everyone. We could be in a waiting room and my mom would talk to the person sitting next to her. I thought, "She doesn't know her, why is she doing that?"

Perhaps it's a maturity thing.

It was not until I was much older that I realized that my mom understood, "We are only visiting, so add as much value as you can, while you can."

For my mom it was about validating the other person—her own version of "I see you and you have value."

It took me many years to figure that out. It wasn't the conversation, it was the human interaction.

I picked up where my mom left off. I talk to or at least acknowledge every person I meet. It may be a simple hello or even a nod. I am dismayed at the number of people I encounter who do not respond, head down and straight ahead. I don't understand why. I know for some they may not hear or see the acknowledgment. But that can't be every case. Some are simply refusing to acknowledge a kindness extended, a recognition of them as humans. No judgment; I just do not get it.

Even the most annoying people deserve a kind word and acknowledgment of their value.

I suggest taking every opportunity to say hello and look for ways to find value in every person and interaction. Look for the good, it's in all of us. We may have to cut through some stuff to find it, but it is worth the effort.

- Value the other person
- A simple hello is enough to acknowledge the existence of another person and may make the difference in another's life.

Time to reflect:
Do your best, in every situation, to leave it better than you found it. After all, we are only visiting.

Act like a dog

I love dogs. As goofy and as stubborn they may be, dogs have life figured out. Cats just do not care.

All dogs need is food, water, a nice place to sleep, some exercise, and someone to love them. That is it.

- Dogs are humble
  - ~ Dogs aren't concerned if they have the most stylish leash.
  - ~ Most would rather not have a leash. Dogs are at their most free when they are off-leash running and enjoying life.
- Dogs only want to play.
  - ~ Watch a dog chasing a ball, stick, or Frisbee. The look of pure joy, excitement, and pleasure as they fetch the ball and drop it at your feet and impatiently wait for the next throw is undeniable.
- Dogs only want to please.
  - ~ Look into a dog's eyes. You'll find inquisitiveness and an earnest "Am I doing it right?"
- Dog's want you to like them; they want to know if you're happy.
  - ~ Dogs get their happiness through you.
- Dogs don't care how big your house is.
  - ~ Self explanatory
- Dogs don't care what kind of car you drive.
  - ~ Same as above
- Dogs don't care what you do for a living.
  - ~ True
- Dogs don't hold grudges
  - ~ This dog attribute is one the most admirable dog attributes.
  - ~ If we use harsh words with our dog, he may sulk or look away. But as soon as we say "It is OK" or "You are a good dog," all is forgiven and they are ready for the next throw, walk, or pat.

- Dogs apologize
  ~ Dogs are intuitive. They know when they have made a mistake and they apologize.
  ~ If your dog has eaten something they should not have or perhaps left a mess, they know.
  ~ We may find them behind the couch or in a corner with that "I let you down" look. Dogs are harder on themselves than we ever could be.
- Dogs tell you how they feel. We just need to look and listen.
  ~ Our dog is old and has a bad heart. We know by his breathing or demeanor how he is feeling.
  ~ Fritz, our dog, does not work and play well with other dogs. He is a Schnauzer/Poodle mix and far more Schnauzer than Poodle. He is the boss, or so he thinks.
  ~ When our daughter and her fiancé visit they bring their dog who loves everybody and every dog. Fritz is not a fan. Fritz literally runs away from home when their dog comes. He puts his little head down and slowly walks down our driveway, turns right and slowly walks down our road. I have to go get him and bring him back. I have to carry him. Now when they visit, Fritz gets a vacation at my wife's parents' house. He is spoiled.
  ~ I believe dogs are great judges of character. They can read people better than we can. We have a neighbor who Fritz absolutely loves. As soon as he sees her, his excitement bubbles over.
- Dogs "Give love away."
  ~ The best thing about dogs, or at least most dogs, is their unconditional love. Our daughter's dog loves everyone. Everyone.
  ~ When we visit or she brings him to our house, we all know Monty is there.
  ~ He greets us all and exudes happiness and joy. He is genuinely happy to see us.
  ~ Even the most shy dogs or older dogs have their "people." These are ones they love to be around and only want to please.
  ~ Dogs don't care if you are right or wrong. Dogs only care about playing, sleeping, and eating. They have no time for right or wrong or whose bowl is bigger.

Fritz, aka, beans, old bean, ding dong, bing bong. But more than anything, my best friend.

October 15 6:45 AM

More wag less bark
More light less dark

More kind less bite
More happy less fight

Helping not selfish
Good thoughts not a bad wish

I try to be like a dog
Happy wags, sleep like a log

No grudges in their day
Only treats and play

Have a beauty day

Love you both give em hell

Mark Twain wrote a short piece many years ago titled, *The Damned Human Race*. He argues that human beings can learn much from the animal world. If you have not read it, you should.

Twain offers many examples.

As long as animals are fed and happy, they will not attack each other. They only are aggressive toward others when provoked, defensive, or hungry. Twain argues animals do not assault each other.

He argues that humans are the only species that kill for sport. That other species only take what they need and use all they can; little goes to waste. His observation stands in stark contrast to the bison hunters in the west who nearly exterminated the once mighty herds and thereby nearly exterminated the native people who relied on every part of the animal for survival. The white hunters only killed these magnificent animals for their hides or trophy.

Think of the native tribes of the American plains who literally lived and died based on the bison and their movement—how their world was devastated as white settlers moved west and began farming and fencing in land. The settlers saw the bison as an obstacle to be conquered or eliminated, not as a source of life for those living in the same area for thousands of years.

I can't imagine the disgust of the native tribes who revered the bison and used every part of the animal and understood the symbiotic relationship of nature. What we do to one, we eventually do to all.

They must have known that their way of life was coming to an end as they saw the bison slaughtered for their hide.

Twain also discusses religion and how animals do not have religion and therefore have far less troubles. Twain says if you put a priest, a rabbi, and cleric in a cage and come back three days later, only one will be left.

Twain forces us to reflect on who we are, what we value and how we live our values.

We can learn much from the animal world.
- Take only what you need.
- Only fight if you must defend yourself as self-defense is a natural right.
- Know that we all are in this world together and any upset in one species upsets all species. If the balance in nature is upset then Mother Nature finds a way to right the wrong. We may not always agree with Mother Nature, but we are at her mercy.

And we might also take a few lessons from dogs: Eat, be humble, sleep, do not hold a grudge, play, apologize, and let others know how you feel. Even more importantly, wag more and bark less.

Time to reflect:
Love your dog (or cat), even though they may have a different agenda.

Be a warrior

I began this writing with a quote from Sitting Bull, the great Hunkpapa Sioux leader. It is a quote I know well and aspire to live. Warriors do not need weapons that destroy. Warriors carry tools that build.

- A warrior is the volunteer who shows up, does their assigned task, does it well and never mentions it again.

- A warrior is the firefighter who risks their life running into a burning building to rescue the animals left behind while all others are running for safety.

- A warrior is the person standing toe-to-toe, unarmed, demanding law enforcement officials remember their oath only to be maced from six inches away and have an arm broken by the people sworn to defend the constitution. And not fight back.

- A warrior is Malala Yousafzai.

- A warrior is the young man who chased down the rapist and held him until the police arrived.

- A warrior is the person who says "I have had enough" and puts down the needle and asks for help to get clean.

- A warrior is my dad who sacrificed to make sure his family had everything we needed.

- A warrior is my mom who took care of three very sick people and never, not once, complained.

- A warrior is my sister Sally and her husband Jon who spent countless hours and countless dollars caring for the most vulnerable creatures.

- A warrior is that young woman who finally finds the courage to tell her parents that she was sexually assaulted.

We often confuse soldiers for warriors.

I have worn the clothing of a soldier and carried the weapons soldiers carry. I was not a warrior. Warriors question, warriors push back and question those who wrong others - human or animal. Warriors do their best to do what is right, never for glory or recognition, only for the good.

I remember a parade in San Angelo, Texas…. I hate parades.

I was part of a tactical platoon. Several other young soldiers and I spent weekends practicing infantry maneuvers and tactics and squad and platoon movements in simulated hostile situations. This parade was a chance to show off our training. We were in a flying V formation. Think geese flying in a V. I was the soldier in the V, the last soldier on the left side of the formation, closest to the people sitting and watching the parade.

We were only using hand signals to communicate. The squad leader raised his left hand in a fist. We stopped. He then swiftly brought his left arm in a downward motion. We went to a knee and brought our M16s up to the ready position.

That is when it happened.

My training taught me to bring my rifle to my shoulder, looking out of the side of the right eye for any further hand commands. When I kneeled, I picked a spot where no one was standing, or so I thought.

In a split second, what was a chance to show off our skills became a terrifying ordeal for a three-year-old boy and a 20-year-old soldier.

138

I heard a shriek and immediately looked down the barrel of the rifle. The muzzle of my M16 was only inches from the face of the three year old. I never saw the child. He and his mom had stepped onto the open space just as I knelt. I never saw them. I immediately pulled the rifle back and moved away from the child and sidewalk. Apologizing the whole time.

I heard the mother say to the child, "It's OK, he is a soldier, he is good, you are OK."

I don't think he was OK. I wasn't OK. I was shaken. I can still see his face and hear the noise of the parade around me. Perhaps it was at that moment that I figured out that the ARMY may not be the right career for me.

Maybe it was that moment I subconsciously decided I was better off as a warrior, not a soldier. This was a defining moment.

Time to reflect:
Look for ways to lead the life that Sitting Bull describes.
Everyday do something for someone else, something they may not be able to do for themselves. Seek out good and make it better. At the end of your day, ask yourself, "Did I make today better than yesterday? Did I make a positive impact for myself or someone else? Did I add value?"

It's your life
Drive or be driven

Former New York State Governor Mario Cuomo (1983 - 1994) said, "Most of life is just a matter of showing up."

I add, for a complete life, show up and engage. You cannot hit a home run if you don't go to the game, you can't hit the high note if you don't go to the concert, you can't score the winning goal if you don't show up to the match. You can not help save a life, if you do not show up. So show up and be engaged in life. We decide if we will show up and we also decide whether we will engage when we do.

We have two options: we can choose to be the driver of our own lives or we can choose to be driven. I encourage you to show up and be present; engage and seek ways to make a positive impact while paying attention to what's happening in the world around you. It all begins with showing up.

You can ride or drive
Wither or thrive

Sit it out and life passes by
Get in the game and you fly

Do all you can to help out
Speak softly no shout

You are the one who makes it so
Be the spark and glow

Have a beauty day

Love you both give em hell

I remember an incident in college that really helped me understand this. I chose to attend college in Florida, 1200 miles away from family and friends. The college planned a trip to Disney World as part of orientation. I went on the trip and literally sat on a bench for about eight hours, lamenting my choice of college, wondering why no one came to me and asked me to go on rides. I was feeling very sorry for myself.

I called my parents that evening when we returned and complained about college, the trip, and most anything else I could think of.

My mom responded, "You chose this."

She was right. Those three words took me from the passenger seat of life and reminded me that I was the driver.

It took me a while to make my way; first years of college can be tough. No excuses though. I was at Disney World, the "happiest place on earth," and I was miserable solely because I made myself so.

Recently, I was volunteering at our local COVID vaccination site. My wife and I were responsible for helping anyone who may need a wheelchair for assistance to get through the process. When we arrived, my wife noticed that all the wheelchairs were kept inside, behind the check-in desk. She said, "This makes no sense" and grabbed two wheel chairs and took them outside. I grabbed two more. She was driving the situation.

About 45 minutes into our volunteer time, a car pulled up and a person inside indicated they needed a wheelchair. I went over and thought it was the older woman in the back of the car that needed assistance. I was wrong. I took the wheelchair to the back door and out popped this spry woman. I watched as she began pulling her brother out of the car.

He had multiple disabilities, no use of his arms and no use of his severely twisted legs. I know very little about physical disabilities, but I did know this was as severe as it could get. This amazing man also had serious cognitive and verbal limitations. Or at least I thought.

I now thought the wheelchair was for her brother. Wrong again, it was for both of them.

She hoisted her brother up and sat back in the chair, holding him as gently as if he were a baby, and talking to him as she would any other adult. They were talking. Not in any way I could understand, but they were talking.

I pushed the chair through the different stations, I realized they were driving—not the chair—they were driving life. They were choosing to engage, not to sit idly by and let things happen to them.

I was amazed and humbled. I witnessed the most genuine act of love. Here was a sister caring and thoroughly enjoying her brother who had every strike against him. She was his protector; he had no better champion. I was in awe.

I saw a story recently of a man hiking the Appalachian Trail. He was diagnosed with Parkinson's and decided he would choose how to live his life. He would not sit and wait for life to happen to him. He was driving.

These are the warriors of which Sitting Bull speaks.

My dad made the decision to drive. He chose to end his life on his terms: "One part doc, make it count." We all knew how it would end. He knew and he made the decision.

My older sister, Holly, was also the driver of her life. She had ovarian cancer. She fought it for two years and we all thought she had beat it. It came back with a vengeance. For a long time we did not know it, she did not tell anyone.

We met her, her boyfriend, her daughter and our mom at a restaurant to celebrate Christmas. It would be her last.

I remarked to my wife on our drive home from that lunch in Rochester how at ease Holly was. She was full of joy. She radiated happiness. I believe she knew her cancer was back and had made her mind up that she was going to let go of this world on her terms. Not pumped full of poison, trying to get one more day out of her already failing body.

She told us all after the holidays. Her cancer was back and she had begun treatment.

After about five weeks of treatments, my mom was helping her get ready for her next chemo appointment when Holly told her, "I am not going." My mom said "OK."

My mom understood and accepted her decision, both of them were warriors.

I enjoyed every call with my sister. We laughed often and each time we hung up from the call, I was reminded how much I was in awe of her, and then I would cry.

The woman and her brother, the man on the Appalachian Trail, my dad, my mom, and Holly. They were drivers. They never complained, they engaged, laughed, never complained and never quit; they fought in their own ways.

As you face the challenges life throws at you, you will have to choose. Will you drive life or let life drive you like it did me in Florida in 1982? Will you take every opportunity to seize life? Will you make decisions and move forward or let hard decisions rock your foundation and make you crumble?

It all begins when you decide to show up.

Another chance to add
To be happy not sad

This is your life. Drive
Find things that make you thrive

Keep it simple and plain
More sun less rain

Only you decide where you go
Only you know

Accept where you are
Or go for a drive. Jump in a car

Have a beauty day

Love you both give em hell

I chose the word "Forward" at the beginning of this writing for this very reason. Keep moving forward as we cannot go back.

A funny note. The very first bracelet I engraved, said "Keep Fucking Moving." One of my students asked me the next day about it as I was wearing it. She asked what I engraved on it. This was a more quiet and reserved student, but so kind. I showed her the engraving and she said, "I want one of those!" OK, so now what to do?

I took the bracelet off and dropped it on the floor. I then picked it up and asked her if she had dropped her bracelet? She laughed and answered, "Yes" and I handed it to her. She smiled and slipped it on her wrist.

That was three years ago and she continues to wear it today.

Almost, but never quite done...

As I wrap up these nearly 44,000 or so words. I recognize that I am who I am not because of the things I have done or achieved. I have succeeded because others sacrificed. I can never know all the sacrifices my parents made for me. I do know there were many.

On my path through life I also learned many things:

- Anger is poison.

- Chasing the arsonist is a loser.

- My "Why" moment hit me at the most unexpected of times and so too will yours. Embrace it and let your "Why" drive you.

- The most beautiful flower can spring from the muck and crap. No mud No Lotus.

- Knowing your role gives you more opportunities than you ever knew existed.

- Admitting and accepting your mistakes will help mold you into a more genuine person.

- I am responsible for myself and my own actions. I understand my actions have consequences, good or bad.

- Maybe I am not as good as I thought. There is always room for improvement.

- What is the worst that can happen?

- Empower, allow, and encourage our children to be genuinely happy in who they truly are.
  - A former teacher had a sign above his desk. It read: "Children do not need better education, children need better childhoods." Dale Tanner

- I have a responsibility to intervene and to protect others.

- Life is best measured through little victories.

- People are weather: we cannot control the weather but we can prepare for it.

- Life is not a game. Do not keep score.

- Always give love away freely and with no expectation of it being returned. Practice Maitri.

- Know and find your Zen.

- Always take care of the people who take care of your people.

- Signing "The goddamn paper" was the right thing to do. I would do it again and when it is my time I trust my wife and children will sign the paper.

- Sometimes the thing we want to do least is the very thing that must be done.

At the same time I wonder:

- Have I lived up to the "Good Man" label my dad bestowed upon me?
- Did I take good care of my mother?
- At any point did I "break my children?"

I can't know these answers. I must believe that I did OK.

I also wonder what being a "Good Man" really means.

My dad was a great mechanic, he could fix anything. In his towing business, he used geometry to extract cars from trees, over cliffs, upside down, in ponds.

He envisioned how the car came to rest in the place it did and used that insight to pull it out largely in the same manner as it went in. It was cool to watch him figure it out. He tried to explain it to me on several occasions. It was math. I didn't get it.

He was not a good businessman.

I remember the numerous times I heard a customer say to him, "George, I am a bit short this week, can I take the car and catch up with you next week?"

His reply was always the same, "Sure, get it to me when you have it."

I asked him once about it and he said that he knew what it was like to be in that situation and "how could he not help someone when they were down?" He also said, and this made complete sense, "How can they get to work if they don't have a car?"

I also asked him what happens if they do not pay him back?

He responded, "They have to live with that."

He knew bad things happen to good people and the best you can do is help them. Trust that they will repay the debt.

I had it wrong; he was a great businessman.
Never fail to be kind

It comes back I find

Anger and hate can bind
Worse yet, they can blind

Do not delay when asked
Most honestly need your help so jump to the task

Never withhold your love
Let it fall as from above

You can add or you can take
It is in the decisions you make

Choose wisely as it determines
Seeds of compassion or vermin

Have a beauty day

Love you both give em hell

Both my mom and dad lived lives of service:

My dad served through the ARMY, police, and by extending grace to people when they needed it.

My mom dedicated a great deal of time to the church. But more than anything she served her kids and her family. I never really understood how tough things were financially on my family largely because of her.

In her later years, my mom took care of three very sick people. She took care of my dad as small vessel disease took away his memory and diabetes attacked his body. She cared for my sister as she fought ovarian cancer and eventually succumbed to it. She visited my brother in the hospital everyday as he recovered from a plane crash, oftentimes going from one hospital to another, part of the day with my sister and part with my brother, with quick stops at their apartment to check on my dad.

Never once in those years did I hear her complain. My mom was a "Good man." I told her that on several occasions. She smiled.

Maybe being a "Good Man" is about service, compassion, and more importantly, empathy. Perhaps being a "Good Man" is about extending a hand to a person when they are down, about handing ten dollars to the guy standing on the street corner with a sign asking for any kind of help, knowing that most of us are one, maybe two missed paychecks away from that very corner.

Perhaps even more, being a "Good man" is simply about kindness with no expectation of reciprocity—Maitri and continually giving love away. Perhaps "Good men" light candles and then hand them off.

As you go about your daily lives, remember….

- Tap the brake.

- Be a "Good Man."

- Give love away.

- Being kind is far more important than being right.

- Be kind to yourself.

- Light candles not fires. peace. andy.

Your last assignment: Buy a bunch of candles, light one with a match and light the rest from the first. Watch how the first can be the light that provides guidance and light for all the others without ever diminishing its flame, beauty and intensity. Be the light for others. Everyday.

Reading List

Throughout this writing I referenced several authors. I encourage you to read them. I found their words make me stronger and able to withstand much of what life sends our way.

Plato's Cave is a must. I reference it at least twice a day. Plato challenges us to break our chains and leave the comfort of what we think we know and challenge us to really know. His writing is more important today than ever.

The Power of Now by Eckhart Tolle. This was the first book I read on being in the present moment. I read it at my lowest point and return to it frequently when confronted by difficult life challenges.

Jon Kabat Zinn is very similar to Tolle, and his book **Wherever You Go There You Are**, offers excellent insight into the mindfulness practice. Zinn takes Tolle a step farther with a deeper understanding and practice.

You are Here by Thich Nhat Hahn. I read this at about the same time as The Power of Now. Hahn provides context and meaning to life's challenges. He offers a nuanced version of life. This was the first book I read by him and have read everything else he has written. When I talk with friends and students who are struggling, I send them a copy of this book.

Welcoming the Unwelcome and **Taking the Leap** by Pema Chodron. Both are excellent in helping us understand that sometimes bad things happen to good people. Chodron provides the reader with tools and thoughts to help soften the blow. Like Hahn, I have read most everything she has written.

For a less philosophical approach to Buddhism with a sound thoughts on everyday life I suggest anything by Timber Hawkeye. His back story is fascinating. You can't go wrong with **Buddhist Bootcamp** or **Faithfully Religionless**.

As I found my footing, I began branching out and exploring different philosophies and life approaches.

Yes to Life and **Man's Search for Meaning** by Viktor Frankl are not just thought provoking, they are also life changing. I will not even try to summarize Frankl's writing. You must read it yourself.

As for Stoicism: Marcus Aurelius' **Meditations** is the go to. Do not be afraid to also read **The Obstacle is the Way** and **The Ego is the Enemy** by Ryan Holiday as he provides everyday examples of Marcus's thoughts on life. Holiday's book **The Daily Stoic** is a day by day reading of Stoic thought in concise and actionable chunks.

Humble the Poet has written a couple of books, similar in style to my writing. I found them by accident when we were visiting our daughter at university in Canada. **Unlearn** and **Things No one Else Can Teach Us** offer a practical approach to being kinder to ourselves.

If you are interested in challenging who you are and what you believe, Ta-Nehisi Coates' **Between the World and Me** opened my eyes to a world I couldn't know until he made me live in it.

James Baldwin. Need I say more. Every time I read him, I realize how much I don't know. As I mentioned in the book, I argue the greatest American socio-political writer EVER.

If you are struggling with end of life decisions Atul Gawnde's **Being Mortal** will provide you with choices that will help make those impossible decisions more manageable.

If you are looking for something to challenge your view on religion, Anthony de Mello is the go to. A Catholic priest, perhaps in name only. Check out **The Way to Love** and **One Minute Wisdom**.

I also read **The Book** by Alan Watts, but in all honesty I struggle with it. I feel like he is playing 3D chess and I am playing tic-tac-toe.

The Prophet by Khalil Gibran is another book I find difficult to comprehend. His prose is beautiful and eloquent. I have read it several times and each time I find something new.

Thank yous

I owe a big debt of gratitude to all the people who have helped me get to this point and writing a complete book. At the top of this list is my wife and two daughters. Their belief in me makes me want to be a better person.

This editing group spent hours reading, rereading, editing, discussing and helping me hone the words and writing to be as sharp, thorough, and concise as possible.

- Thank you, Christine Merritt, for laying out the structure and being my sounding board and providing smart and honest advice on things far more important than this book. You are my Yoda.
- Thank you, Sally Merritt-Braciak, for your hours of editing and writing suggestions and filling in the blanks.
- BIG LOVE to Lori Bedell, for her fine-tooth comb editing. The writing flows due to her work.
- BIG LOVE to Marylou Manhart for your honesty and spot on suggestions.
- Thank you, Matt Lintal, another Yoda, for your honest and thoughtful feedback.
- Thank you, Katrina deRoos-Hatch, for your final fine-tooth look. A fresh set of eyes makes a huge difference. Also, and more importantly, thank you for literally being my life long friend.
- Thank you, Jason Gruhl. Your insight, thoughtful and honest feedback gave me many reasons to think and make this writing the best it can be.
- Thank you, Penny Eifrig and Eifrig Publishing, for taking a chance on me and my writing. Your belief and faith in me is humbling.

CPSIA information can be obtained
at www.ICGtesting.com
Printed in the USA
BVHW081248140222
628721BV00003B/10

9 781632 333261